Hardhatting in a Geo-World

Authors

Betty Cordel	Geraldine Haracz
Barry Courtney	Loretta Hill
Helen Crossley	Ann Wiebe
Susan Dixon	Nancy Williams

Editors

Ann Wiebe
Betty Cordel
Judith Hillen

Illustrators

Reneé Mason
Margo Pocock
Brenda Richmond

Desktop Publisher

Tracey Lieder
Kristy Shuler

This book contains materials developed by the AIMS Education Foundation. **AIMS** (**A**ctivities **I**ntegrating **M**athematics and **S**cience) began in 1981 with a grant from the National Science Foundation. The non-profit AIMS Education Foundation publishes hands-on instructional materials (books and the monthly magazine) that integrate curricular disciplines such as mathematics, science, language arts, and social studies. The Foundation sponsors a national program of professional development through which educators may gain both an understanding of the AIMS philosophy and expertise in teaching by integrated, hands-on methods.

ISBN **1-881431-67-3**

Printed in the United States of America

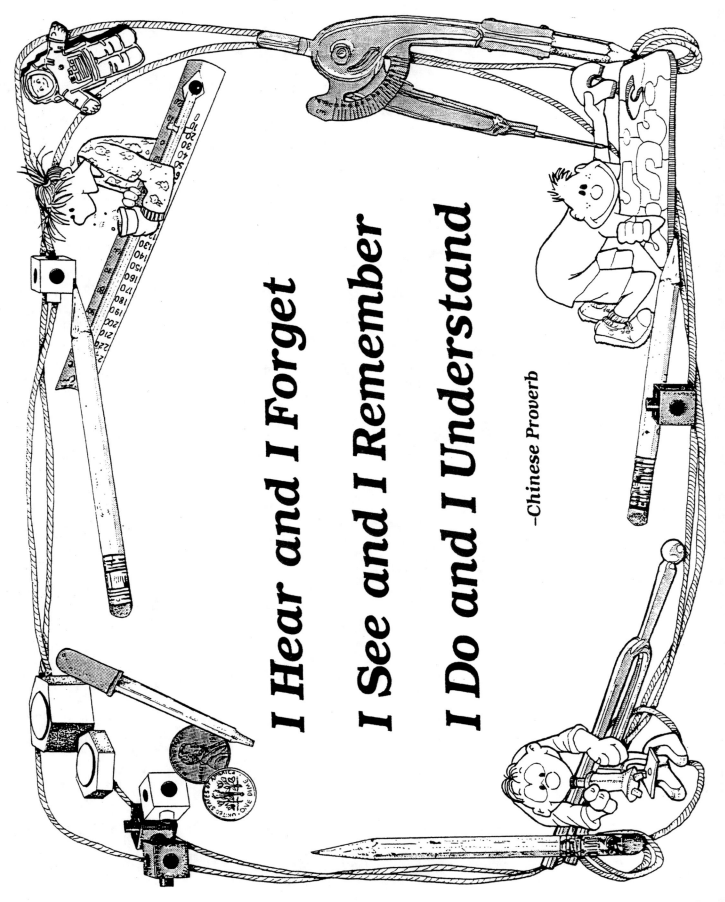

I Hear and I Forget

I See and I Remember

I Do and I Understand

—Chinese Proverb

Table of Contents

MATH	Estimation	Counting	Measurement	Whole number operations	Averages	Ordering	Graphing	Geometry and spatial sense	Problem solving	Patterns
Pillars of Strength	X		X					X		
Working Out the Wiggles								X	X	
Straws Take a Stand								X	X	
Sky High			X		X		X	X		
Thanks For Your Support!			X					X		
Bridge It		X	X					X		
Rulers Line Up			X							
Links to Length	X		X		X		X		X	
Are You a Square?	X		X				X			
Bear Facts	X	X	X	X						
Cups 'n' Stuff	X		X			X	X			
Peddle the Metal			X	X						
Filling Stations			X				X			
Pleased as Punch			X				X			
Minute Minders		X	X							
From Wedges to Wangles			X					X		
Waxed Wangles			X					X	X	
Shaping Up								X		
Slice Me Twice								X		
Möbius Bands		X						X		
Geo-panes		X						X		
Edge to Edge								X		X
Net-Sense								X		
Wreck-Tangles			X			X		X		
Paper Pinchers		X	X					X		X
Circle Sighs			X					X		
Playground Geometry	X		X	X				X		
Once Around the Track								X		X

INTEGRATED PROCESSES

	Predicting	Controlling variables	Observing	Collecting/recording data	Comparing/contrasting	Classifying	Interpreting data	Drawing conclusions	Generalizing	Applying
Pillars of Strength		X	X	X	X				X	X
Working Out the Wiggles			X	X	X				X	
Straws Take a Stand			X		X				X	
Sky High	X		X	X	X					X
Thanks For Your Support!			X	X	X					X
Bridge It			X	X	X					X
Rulers Line Up			X	X	X		X		X	
Links to Length		X	X	X	X					
Are You a Square?			X	X	X	X	X			
Bear Facts			X	X	X					
Cups 'n' Stuff		X	X	X	X			X		
Peddle the Metal			X	X	X					X
Filling Stations	X		X	X	X					
Pleased as Punch		X	X	X	X					
Minute Minders			X	X	X			X		
From Wedges to Wangles			X	X	X	X				
Waxed Wangles			X	X	X					X
Shaping Up			X	X	X	X				
Slice Me Twice	X		X	X	X				X	X
Möbius Bands	X		X	X	X					
Geo-panes	X		X	X	X				X	
Edge to Edge	X		X	X	X					
Net-Sense	X		X	X	X					
Wreck-Tangles			X	X	X				X	
Paper Pinchers	X		X	X	X				X	
Circle Sighs			X	X	X		X	X		
Playground Geometry			X	X	X	X				
Once Around the Track			X	X	X				X	

*Project 2061 Benchmarks**

The Nature of Science
- *Results of scientific investigations are seldom exactly the same, but if the differences are large, it is important to try to figure out why. One reason for following directions carefully and for keeping records of one's work is to provide information on what might have caused the differences.*

The Nature of Mathematics
- *Mathematical ideas can be represented concretely, graphically, and symbolically.*
- *Mathematics is the study of many kinds of patterns, including numbers and shapes and operations on them. Sometimes patterns are studied because they help to explain how the world works or how to solve practical problems, sometimes because they are interesting in themselves.*
- *Numbers and shapes—and operations on them—help to describe and predict things about the world around us.*

The Nature of Technology
- *Measuring instruments can be used to gather accurate information for making scientific comparisons of objects and events and for designing and constructing things that will work properly.*
- *Even a good design may fail. Sometimes steps can be taken ahead of time to reduce the likelihood of failure, but it cannot be entirely eliminated.*
- *Scientific laws, engineering principles, properties of materials, and construction techniques must be taken into account in designing engineering solutions*
to problems. Other factors, such as cost, safety, appearance, environmental impact, and what will happen if the solution fails also must be considered.*

The Mathematical World
- *When people care about what is being counted or measured, it is important for them to say what the units are (three degrees Fahrenheit is different from three centimeters, three miles from three miles per hour).*
- *Measurements are always likely to give slightly different numbers, even if what is being measured stays the same.*
- *Tables and graphs can show how values of one quantity are related to values of another.*
- *Length can be thought of as unit lengths joined together, area as a collection of unit squares, and volume as a set of unit cubes.*
- *Graphical display of numbers may make it possible to spot patterns that are not otherwise obvious, such as comparative size and trends.*

- *Shapes such as circles, squares, and triangles can be used to describe many things that can be seen.*
- *Many objects can be described in terms of simple plane figures and solids. Shapes can be compared in terms of concepts such as parallel and perpendicular, congruence and similarity, and symmetry. Symmetry can be found by reflection, turns, or slides.*

- Some shapes have special properties: Triangular shapes tend to make structures rigid, and round shapes give the least possible boundary for a given amount of interior area. Shapes can match exactly or have the same shape in different sizes.
- Spreading data out on a number line helps to see what the extremes are, where they pile up, and where the gaps are. A summary of data includes where the middle is and how much spread is around it.

Common Themes
- Some features of things may stay the same even when other features change. Some patterns look the same when they are shifted over, or turned, or reflected, or seen from different directions.

Habits of Mind
- Keep records of their investigations and observations and not change the records later.
- Offer reasons for their findings and consider reasons suggested by others.
- Add, subtract, multiply, and divide whole numbers mentally, on paper, and with a calculator.
- Judge whether measurements and computations of quantities such as length, area, volume, weight, or time are reasonable in a familiar context by comparing them to typical values.

- Assemble, describe, take apart and reassemble constructions using interlocking blocks, erector sets, and the like.
- Make something out of paper, cardboard, wood, plastic, metal, or existing objects that can actually be used to perform a task.
- Measure and mix dry and liquid materials (in the kitchen, garage, or laboratory) in prescribed amounts, exercising reasonable safety.
- Make sketches to aid in explaining procedures or ideas.
- Use numerical data in describing and comparing objects and events.

*American Association for the Advancement of Science. **Benchmarks for Science Literacy.** Oxford University Press. New York. 1993.

NRC Standards*

Abilities necessary to do scientific inquiry
- Plan and conduct a simple investigation.
- Employ simple equipment and tools to gather data and extend the senses.
- Use data to construct a reasonable explanation.
- Communicate investigations and explanations.

Properties of objects and materials
- Objects have many observable properties, including size, weight, shape, color, temperature, and the ability to react with other substances. Those properties can be measured using tools, such as rulers, balances, and thermometers.

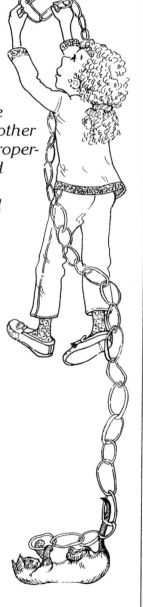

Abilities of technological design
- Identify a simple problem.
- Propose a solution.
- Implementing proposed solutions.
- Evaluate a product or design.
- Communicate a problem, design, and solution.

Understanding about science and technology
- Tools help scientists make better observations, measurements, and equipment for investigations. They help scientists see, measure, and do things that they could not otherwise see, measure, and do.

* National Research Council. **National Science Education Standards.** National Academy Press. Washington, DC. 1996.

NCTM Standards*

Mathematics as Communication
- *Relate physical materials, pictures, and diagrams to mathematical ideas*

Mathematics as Reasoning
- *Use patterns and relationships to analyze mathematical situations*

Mathematical Connections
- *Apply mathematical thinking and modeling to solve problems that arise in other disciplines, such as art, music, psychology, science, and business*

Estimation
- *Apply estimation in working with quantities, measurement, computation, and problem solving*

Whole Number Computation
- *Select and use computation techniques appropriate to specific problems and determine whether the results are reasonable*

Geometry and Spatial Sense
- *Describe, model, draw, and classify shapes*
- *Investigate and predict the results of combining, subdividing, and changing shapes*
- *Explore transformations of geometric figures*
- *Develop spatial sense*
- *Relate geometric ideas to number and measurement ideas*
- *Recognize and appreciate geometry in their world*

Measurement
- *Understand the attributes of length, capacity, weight, mass, area, volume, time, temperature, and angle*
- *Develop the process of measuring and concepts related to units of measurement*
- *Make and use measurements in problems and everyday situations*

Statistics
- *Collect, organize, and describe data*
- *Construct, read, and interpret displays of data*

* *National Council of Teachers of Mathematics.* **Curriculum and Evaluation Standards for School Mathematics.** *The National Council of Teachers of Mathematics, Inc. Reston, Virginia. 1989.*

Pillars of STRENGTH

Topic
Strength of paper tubes

Key Questions
1. How can we make a stronger paper tube?
2. Challenge: Build a paper tube, at least 3 cm tall, that will support a person.

Focus
Students will explore how height, diameter, and thickness affect the strength of a paper tube. They will then build a paper tube that will support a person.

Guiding Documents
Project 2061 Benchmarks
- *Measuring instruments can be used to gather accurate information for making scientific comparisons of objects and events and for designing and constructing things that will work properly.*
- *Make something out of paper, cardboard, wood, plastic, metal, or existing objects that can actually be used to perform a task.*
- *Make sketches to aid in explaining procedures or ideas.*

NRC Standards
- *Employ simple equipment and tools to gather data and extend the senses.*
- *Evaluate a product or design.*
- *Communicate a problem, design, and solution.*

NCTM Standard
- *Make and use measurements in problems and everyday situations*

Math
Estimation
Measurement
    length
Geometry and spatial sense

Science
Physical science
    force

Technology
Engineering
    structures

Integrated Processes
Observing
Collecting and recording data
Identifying and controlling variables
Comparing and contrasting
Generalizing
Applying

Materials
Used copy paper
Tape
Hardback books (see *Management*)
Metric rulers

Background Information
Tubes are hollow and light, yet resist bending or twisting. They can stand alone or be part of a larger framework. Tubes used for strength are found in nature (plant stems, bones, etc.) and made by people (bicycle frames, metal ladder rungs, buildings, freeways, bridges, etc.). They are used in both horizontal and vertical positions, singularly or bundled.

Variables of height, diameter, thickness, material used, position (horizontal or vertical), and whether single or bundled determine the degree of support possible. Thick walls have more structural strength than thin walls. A larger diameter provides greater support because the mass is distributed over a larger area. Theoretically, the height of the tubes would not matter if they could always be kept truly vertical; however, in the real world, a taller tube is more likely to be off-vertical. This weakens the structure and causes it to collapse.

Management
1. For this activity, the variables of position (vertical), kind of paper (copy paper), and number of tubes (single rather than multiple) are controlled. Students explore height, diameter, and thickness.
2. Collect used copy paper so that plenty is available.
3. It is important to use identical books for the strength test. Identify a particular textbook, dictionary, etc. to be used.
4. To conduct the strength test, construct a tube, place it vertically on a smooth, flat surface, and carefully center a book on top of it. Keep adding books, one at a time, until the tube is crushed.

Count the number of books it supported, minus the one that caused it to fall. It is not a fair test if a book imbalance caused the tube to crush.

5. Groups of two or three are suggested.

6. To control the variable of mass when doing *Step On It*, a single person (teacher or student) should be chosen for the final test of all the tubes. Center a book (or clipboard) over the tube and have a person stand on top of the book with one foot, using a chair or another person to maintain balance.

7. The activity is divided into two parts, exploration (*Pillars of Strength*) and application (*Step On It*). These can be done on two separate days or for a longer period on one day. Consider using *Step On It* for assessment.

The following approach is offered for those students ready for more independent exploration.

> *Open-ended:* Ask the *Key Question* and explain the materials available to the groups. Let them plan their own procedure for exploring and reporting on this question. Then challenge them to build a paper tube that will support a person.

Procedure

1. Hold up a piece of used copy paper and ask, "How can we make a tube out of this?" Have students demonstrate their ideas.

2. Ask the *Key Question*, "How can we make a stronger paper tube?"

3. Have students think of different ways to change the tube (variables) as they explore this question. Once the variables have been identified, distribute the first activity sheet.

4. Review together how to conduct the strength test. Demonstrate, if needed.

5. Guide the discussion about the first variable to be tested, height. Ask, "What other variables cannot change during this test?" [diameter, thickness] The class or each group will need to decide what those standards will be. It is best to initially work with a single thickness of paper.

6. Instruct students to record the estimate of the number of books their best tube (during the three sets of tests) will support.

7. Have students perform the tests and record their data. They should record their best test result next to the estimate. You may wish to pause between each test for a discussion about the previous test and controlling variables for the next test. For example, students may reason that they should use the most successful tube height as the controlled height during the diameter test.

8. Have the groups report and compare their results.

9. Based on the data they have gathered, challenge students to build a paper tube that will support a person.

10. Distribute the *Step On It* activity sheet and explain how it is to be completed. Turn students loose to be creative engineers.

11. Have the chosen person test each group's tube. Students should compare the results, both in appearance and in performance.

Discussion

1. What different ways can we build tubes from a piece of paper? [change the height, the diameter, the thickness, the kind of material, etc.]

2. You've just finished the _____ (name a variable) test. What was your strongest tube? Why do you think it was the strongest?

3. Look at the information from all of your tests. What combination would you use to construct the strongest possible tube?

4. How does your group's information compare with others in the class?

5. How did you use the data from *Pillars of Strength* to design the tube that supports a person?

6. How do the different groups' tubes that support a person compare in the way they look? ...in the way they perform their job?

7. How are tubes used in construction for support? (This may lead to searches for pictures in books or a walking field trip around the school or community.)

8. You are constructing a building with some tall pillars that need to support a lot of mass. Describe the pillars you would want to use. [They should be thick and have large diameters.]

Extensions

1. Have each group find the mass of the books supported by their strongest tube on the first activity sheet. This might involve some problem solving.

2. Try other kinds of paper for making strong tubes.

3. Investigate the strength of attaching several tubes together (bundling).

4. Have students devise a plan for exploring the strength of tubes used as horizontal beams.

Pillars of STRENGTH

How can we make a stronger paper tube?

THE STRENGTH TEST
Place books on the tube, one
at a time, until it collapses.

How many books will your
best tube support?
_____   _____
Estimate   Actual

Test each variable and record the results below.

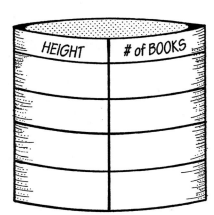

HEIGHT	# of BOOKS

KEEP THE SAME
Diameter: _____ cm
Thickness: <u>1 sheet</u>

DIAMETER	# of BOOKS

KEEP THE SAME
Height: _____ cm
Thickness: <u>1 sheet</u>

THICKNESS	# of BOOKS

KEEP THE SAME
Height: _____ cm
Diameter: _____ cm

STEP ON IT

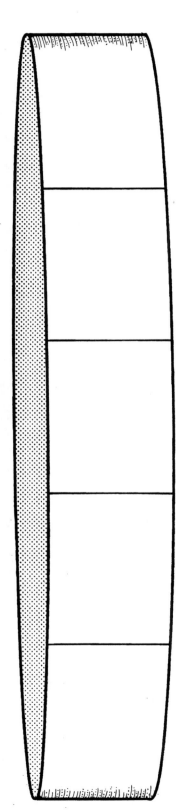

1. Build a paper tube, at least 3 cm tall, that will support a person.

2. Change and retest the tube until you are satisfied.

CONSTRUCTION LOG

Draw and describe the tube each time it is changed.

Compare your tube to others in the class.

Working Out the Wiggles

Topic
Stability of various polygons

Key Question
How can we make a structure stable?

Focus
Students will construct, test, and find ways to stabilize various polygons. They will discover that the triangle is the basis of a stable structure.

Guiding Documents
Project 2061 Benchmarks
- *Some shapes have special properties: Triangular shapes tend to make structures rigid, and round shapes give the least possible boundary for a given amount of interior area. Shapes can match exactly or have the same shape in different sizes.*
- *Assemble, describe, take apart and reassemble constructions using interlocking blocks, erector sets, and the like.*

NRC Standards
- *Identify a simple problem.*
- *Evaluate a product or design.*
- *Communicate a problem, design, and solution.*

NCTM Standards
- *Relate physical materials, pictures, and diagrams to mathematical ideas*
- *Describe, model, draw, and classify shapes*
- *Apply mathematical thinking and modeling to solve problems that arise in other disciplines, such as art, music, psychology, science, and business*

Math
Geometry
Problem solving

Science
Physical science
force

Technology
Engineering
structures

Integrated Processes
Observing
Collecting and recording data
Comparing and contrasting
Generalizing

Materials
For the class:
several hole punches
scissors

For each group:
6 tagboard strips, 2 cm x 10 cm
3 tagboard strips, 2 cm x 20 cm
6 paper fasteners

Background Information
The triangle is the only polygon which is rigid. All the sides push against each other to hold it in a stable position. The length of at least two sides would have to be changed in order for the triangle to move laterally. Triangles are commonly incorporated into the basic design of (or used to brace) buildings, towers, roofs, roller coasters, bridges, and many other kinds of structures made by people.

In this activity, students discover the stability of the triangle as they explore ways to make squares, pentagons, and hexagons rigid. Some possible solutions are shown below.

Square   Pentagon   Hexagon

Management
1. Construct one of the polygons beforehand to determine the size of paper fastener needed for the holes made by the hole punches. Small (1/8") hole punches work very well with No. 2, 1/2" paper fasteners. But use the hole punch size most easily available to you because the quantity of hole punches, in most cases, is more important than size in this activity.
2. If you have a limited number of hole punches, prepare the tagboard strips by punching holes in both ends of the 10 cm strips and in one end of the 20 cm strips.

3. Have extra paper fasteners and 2 cm x 20 cm tagboard strips available as groups guess and test different bracing possibilities.
4. Groups of two work best.
5. Making a structure stable may involve several tries before success is achieved. Encourage students to persist until they reach their goal.

(The following is offered for those students ready for more independent investigation.)

Open-ended: Illustrate the tagboard/paper fastener construction. Brainstorm shapes to try and discuss the meaning of *stable*. Introduce the *Key Question* and have students plan how they will record and report their discoveries. There should be evidence that they have studied the results and drawn conclusions. They might also generate questions to be answered.

Procedure
1. Join two 10-cm tagboard strips with a paper fastener and show this to the class. Explain that they will be building different shapes from these materials and finding which ones are stable. Tell them that *stable* means it will not move from side to side.
2. Give each group the tagboard strips, paper fasteners, and activity sheet. Have hole punches, extra strips, and extra paper fasteners available.
3. Instruct students to build one shape at a time with the 10 cm strips and draw a picture of it in the row labeled *Structure*.
4. Students should brace the shape, if needed, and complete the column in the table. To brace, they should attach a longer strip to the desired location, move it into position, mark where the second hole needs to be made, and punch a hole at this mark. Caution them not to trim the strip because they will use it again. (Bracing will probably be a trial-and-error experience. Encourage students to keep trying until they find a way that works.)
5. Direct students to take each structure apart and use the same materials for the next one.
6. When they have completed the table, give them time to study their drawings and answer the two questions. Let students determine a way to compare the number of sides and braces. (For example, they could make a table.)
7. Hold a concluding discussion.

Discussion
1. What way(s) did you find to build the new shapes faster? [Don't take the whole shape apart. For example, just open up the triangle, add one more strip, and you have a square.]

2. When was bracing most difficult? [at the beginning (square) when I didn't know what worked, maybe at the end (hexagon) because it got more complicated]
3. How did the way you braced the square compare with other groups? Did more than one way work?
4. What is similar about all the square braces? [They divide the square into two regions, the endpoints are on adjoining strips.] Which brace do you think is strongest? [the one on the diagonal]
5. What ways did you try to brace the square that did not work? (Have students reflect on their guess-and-test process. Remind them that scientists experience many failures before they have a success.) *Repeat questions 3-5 for the pentagon and the hexagon.*
6. What do all the stable structures have in common? [They form triangles.]
7. How might this information be useful in construction? How might an engineer use this information for a building, a tower, or a bridge? [They should use triangles when they design these structures.]
8. How do the number of sides and the number of braces compare? Is there a pattern? If so, what is it? (If students make a table, the pattern is easier to see: number of sides - 3 = number of braces.)

Extensions
1. Take the class on a walk around the neighborhood or the school grounds and look for examples of triangles being used to make stable structures. Have students observe triangles as they walk home from school.
2. Have students collect and examine pictures of bridges, towers, skyscrapers, playground equipment, etc. These may be made into a bulletin board collage.

Curriculum Correlation
Literature
Burns, Marilyn. *The Greedy Triangle.* Scholastic, Inc. NY. 1994.

Home Link
Have students search at home for items, such as toys, that use triangles for strength.

Working Out the Wiggles

How can we make a structure stable?

Structure				
Name of Shape	TRIANGLE	SQUARE	PENTAGON	HEXAGON
Is it stable?				
Show how you made it stable using the fewest braces.				

What do you notice about the stable structures?

How do the number of sides and the number of braces compare?

Constructing With Straws

In order to build straw structures, the straws must be joined together. Several methods for joining are illustrated below. Choose the method that will best work for you, taking into consideration available materials, the manual dexterity of your students, the kind of project, and safety. A combination of methods may be needed for some projects.

INSERTION

Pinch the end of one straw and insert it into another straw. By making slits, straws can be joined in places other than at the ends.

PIPE CLEANERS

Bend short lengths of large pipe cleaners (chenille strips) and insert into the ends of straws. For in-between connections, cut a slit in the straw.

TRANSPARENT TAPE

Join straws by taping. A lot of tape will be needed.

PAPER CLIPS

Link two paper clips together and insert each clip into a straw. Paper clips can also be slid onto a straw for connections that are not on the ends of straws.

PINS

Attach straws by poking with straight pins. This is one of the fastest ways to build or change a structure, but it does raise a safety issue.

Straws Take a Stand

Topic
Stability of a cube

Key Question
How can you make a cube stable?

Focus
Students will build a cube with straws and discover that triangular braces are needed to make it stable.

Guiding Documents
Project 2061 Benchmarks
- *Some shapes have special properties: Triangular shapes tend to make structures rigid, and round shapes give the least possible boundary for a given amount of interior area. Shapes can match exactly or have the same shape in different sizes.*
- *Assemble, describe, take apart and reassemble constructions using interlocking blocks, erector sets, and the like.*

NRC Standards
- *Identify a simple problem.*
- *Propose a solution.*
- *Implementing proposed solutions.*

NCTM Standards
- *Relate physical materials, pictures, and diagrams to mathematical ideas*
- *Describe, model, draw, and classify shapes*
- *Apply mathematical thinking and modeling to solve problems that arise in other disciplines, such as art, music, psychology, science, and business*

Math
Geometry
Problem solving

Science
Physical science
   force

Technology
Engineering
   structures

Integrated Processes
Observing
Comparing and contrasting
Generalizing

Materials
For each group:
   12 straws
   36 paper clips
   scissors

Background Information
The triangle is the basis for stable two- and three-dimensional shapes. It is the only polygon which is rigid. Its position cannot be altered unless the length of a side is changed. The triangle is commonly used in the design and bracing of buildings, towers, roofs, bridges, roller coasters, and many other kinds of structures.

When the cube is constructed in this activity, students will experience its lack of stability. Through trial-and-error experimentation or the application of knowledge previously gained in *Working Out the Wiggles*, students will discover that triangular braces make the cube rigid.

The building of the tetrahedron intentionally follows the building of the cube. After having to add several braces to make the cube stable, students find the tetrahedron needs no such bracing. What's going on here? There may be a pause, then the moment of realization. The tetrahedron is made of triangles! Ahhh...the joy of discovery.

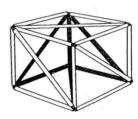

Management
1. Use groups of two or three. Responsibilities might be divided as follows: holding the structure, handling the paper clips, and inserting the straws.
2. For each group, cut six straws in half and leave the other six full-length.
3. Joining straws together can be challenging. One of the easier ways is to join two paper clips and insert each clip into a straw (*Diagram A*). If another paper clip is needed at that vertex, just attach it to the others. The paper clips should fit snugly inside the straws. Since the clips will not be bent open, they can be used for their normal purpose after this activity. Students who wish to try braces other than the diagonal can use the construction technique illustrated in *Diagram B*.

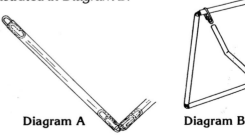

Diagram A   **Diagram B**

Procedure

1. Issue the challenge: Build a stable cube with straws. Explain that stable means that the structure will not move from side to side; it is stiff. Demonstrate the method for joining straws together with paper clips.

2. Distribute the activity sheet, 12 half-length straws, and a starter pile of paper clips to each group. (Don't give students all 36 paper clips as this might provide hints in meeting the challenge. They can get more as they discover the need for them.)

3. Instruct students to build the cube.

4. Ask, "How stable is your cube?" [It is not stable at all.] "Does this surprise you?"

5. Have students continue with the challenge of making the cube stable. Make full-length straws and more paper clips available as they experiment with bracing. Students should cut these additional straws to the length needed.

6. When groups have met the challenge, show them how to draw a cube on the activity sheet.

   a. Darken four dots forming the corners of a 3x3 square. Draw the square.

   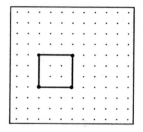

   b. From one dot, move up and over the amount you wish (for example, up 1 and over 1). Repeat this pattern from each of the original dots. Draw another square.

   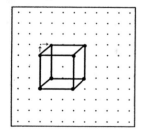

   c. Connect the two squares with lines. Then add brace lines. (Not all brace lines are shown below.)

   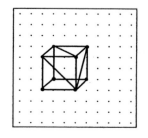

7. Have students describe the shapes in their stable cube on the activity sheet.

8. Instruct students to take the cube apart and build a tetrahedron (illustrated on activity sheet) with the same materials.

9. Hold a concluding discussion and have students generalize by describing their discovery on the activity sheet.

Discussion

1. What helpful construction techniques did you discover?

2. What surprised you? (possibly that the cube was so wobbly without braces, that the tetrahedron didn't need to be braced, etc.)

3. How do the cube and the tetrahedron compare? [One has six sides, the other four sides. The cube was not stable without braces, the tetrahedron was.]

4. What makes a structure stable? [triangles, whether braced or as a part of the original shape]

5. How many triangles were in the cube? [12] How does this relate to the number of sides (faces)? [It is double the number of sides because each brace divides a face into two sections.]

6. How would knowing that triangles make strong structures be helpful to people? [When planning a building, bridge, or tower you want it to be safe for people to use and to do the job for which it was designed.]

7. Can you think of anything at your home that would benefit from being cross-braced? [bookshelves, etc.]

8. You are in charge of getting the materials ready for this activity. How many straws and paper clips do you need for our class? (Students will need to determine the number of groups, then count the materials they used to build and brace the cube. They should remember that some of the straws are cut in half so two half straws started out as one whole straw.)

Extension

Have the class search for structures around them that use triangles for strength: bicycles, playground equipment, etc.

Straws Take a Stand

Challenge: Build a stable cube with straws.

Draw your cube.

What shapes do you see?

Try and build a stable tetrahedron.
Explain what you discovered.

Topic
Tall structures

Key Question
Challenge: Build the tallest structure you can with 30 drinking straws.

Focus
Students will use creativity, teamwork, and problem solving as they build a tall, stable structure.

Guiding Documents
Project 2061 Benchmark
- *Scientific laws, engineering principles, properties of materials, and construction techniques must be taken into account in designing engineering solutions to problems. Other factors, such as cost, safety, appearance, environmental impact, and what will happen if the solution fails also must be considered.*

NRC Standards
- *Identify a simple problem.*
- *Propose a solution.*
- *Implementing proposed solutions.*
- *Evaluate a product or design.*

NCTM Standards
- *Develop spatial sense*
- *Make and use measurements in problems and everyday situations*
- *Construct, read, and interpret displays of data*

Math
Geometry and spatial sense
Measurement
  linear
Graphing
Median average

Science
Physical science
  force

Technology
Engineering
  structures

Integrated Processes
Observing
Predicting
Collecting and recording data
Comparing and contrasting
Applying

Materials
For each group:
  30 plastic straws
  material to join straws (see *Management*)
  clay to anchor structures
  meter sticks

Background Information
    This is one of several activities in which students of all ages can apply the knowledge gained from *Working Out the Wiggles* and *Straws Take a Stand*. Triangular braces add strength. They are needed to make a strong base as well as to support the straw structure as it rises higher and higher.

    If the data are ordered, in this case from shortest height to tallest height, the height in the middle is the median average. This kind of average is more easily understood than the mean average, particularly if the data are presented visually in a graph.

Management
1. Allow 1 to 1 1/2 hours. You may wish to set a time limit of 45-60 minutes for actual construction.
2. Groups of two or three should work together on a structure.
3. Construction should take place on the floor. Use clay to anchor the straw base to the floor. If working on carpet, clay is not needed.

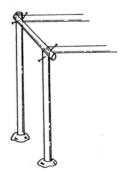

4. Choose one or more methods for connecting straws from the options suggested in *Constructing With Straws* (see *Table of Contents*). Assemble the appropriate materials.

Procedure

1. Issue the *Challenge* and distribute the first activity page to each group (or each student). Have them predict the height of the tallest structure they think will be built.
2. Instruct a member of each group to collect the straws, clay, and other items needed for construction.
3. Show students how to anchor the clay and join straws together.
4. Have students build their structures.
5. Direct students to record their structure's estimated height, then measure its actual height.
6. Tell students to make a drawing of their structure and compare it to the tallest one built.
7. Guide the reporting of height data for all of the structures so students can record on the second activity page.
8. Have students make a bar graph, ordering the data from shortest to tallest. They should mark the middle height to find the median average.
9. Discuss the results.

Discussion

1. How did you change (modify) your structure?
2. How did you use ideas you learned earlier?
3. What advice would you give someone who was going to build a similar structure? (You need a firmly-braced base or foundation. Use triangles whenever possible to strengthen the structure, etc.)
4. What surprised you about the different structures that were built?
5. Do you think a higher straw structure (than the tallest in class) could be built with only 30 straws? How would you plan to do it?
6. If you were to build another straw structure, what would you want the challenge to be?

Sky High

Challenge: Build the highest structure you can using 30 straws.

Design Team

How high do you think the tallest structure will be?

YOUR STRUCTURE

Estimated height _____

Actual height _____

How does your structure compare with the tallest structure built?

Draw your structure.

Sky High

Design Team

Record the heights of all the structures.

Graph the heights, in order, from shortest to tallest. Mark the middle height, the median average.

15

Thanks For Your Support!

Topic
Supporting structures

Key Question
Challenge: Build a structure that will support 400 grams at least 25 cm above the base.

Focus
Students will use creativity, teamwork, and problem solving to build a drinking straw structure which can hold 400 grams of mass.

Guiding Documents
Project 2061 Benchmarks
- *Scientific laws, engineering principles, properties of materials, and construction techniques must be taken into account in designing engineering solutions to problems. Other factors, such as cost, safety, appearance, environmental impact, and what will happen if the solution fails also must be considered.*
- *Even a good design may fail. Sometimes steps can be taken ahead of time to reduce the likelihood of failure, but it cannot be entirely eliminated.*

NRC Standards
- *Identify a simple problem.*
- *Propose a solution.*
- *Implementing proposed solutions.*
- *Evaluate a product or design.*
- *Communicate a problem, design, and solution.*

NCTM Standards
- *Develop spatial sense*
- *Make and use measurements in problems and everyday situations*

Math
Geometry and spatial sense
Measurement
 linear
 mass

Science
Physical science
 force

Technology
Engineering
 structures

Integrated Processes
Observing
Collecting and recording data
Comparing and contrasting
Applying

Materials
For each group:
 30 plastic straws, minimum
 material to join straws (see *Management 4*)
 metric ruler
 empty 16 oz. sour cream or cottage cheese
  container
 material with a mass of 400 grams (see
  Management 5)

For the class:
 balance
 gram masses

Background Information
 This is one of a series of activities that uses plastic drinking straws as the construction medium. The challenge presented requires creativity, cooperation, and problem solving. Students have an opportunity to apply what they have learned in *Working Out the Wiggles* and *Straws Take a Stand*, that triangular braces add strength to a structure. They will also evaluate their structures for cost, safety, and appearance.

One solution

Management
1. *Working Out the Wiggles* and *Straws Take a Stand* are strongly recommended preliminary activities.
2. Divide the class into groups of two or three.
3. Each group should start with 30 straws but have plenty of extras on hand in case they need more. If you wish to set a maximum, it should be at least 40 straws.

4. Choose one or more methods for connecting straws from the options suggested in *Constructing With Straws* (see *Table of Contents*). Assemble the appropriate materials.
5. Collect rocks or other materials that will fit into a sour cream container. Beforehand, measure or have each group measure 400 grams of rocks using the balance and gram masses. The rocks may be a bit over, but not under 400 grams. The rocks will gradually be added to the sour cream container to test the structure.

Procedure
1. Present students with the *Challenge*. Distribute the activity sheet, straws and other materials.
2. Review with the class how to test their structure. Carefully place the container on top of the structure and gently add a few rocks at a time. Solve any weakness problems before adding more mass.
3. Have students build and test their structures.
4. Direct each student or student group to measure the height and amount of mass supported, then draw the structure they built.
5. Ask students to look at the structures of other groups and compare with their own.
6. Discuss the results.

Discussion
1. What changes did you make in your structure as you were building?
2. What do you like about your structure?
3. How did you use ideas you learned earlier?
4. How well did your group work together? Give an example.
5. Which structure has the most pleasing appearance?
6. Which structure appears to be the safest?
7. If each straw costs 10¢, how much did your structure cost to build? (You might assign prices to the other building materials used and have them figure total costs.)
8. If you were on a budget, for which structure would you be willing to pay? Why?

Curriculum Correlation
Language Arts
   Wilson, Forrest. *What It Feels Like To Be A Building.* The Preservation Press, National Trust for Historic Preservation, 1785 Massachusetts Avenue. N.W., Washington, D.C. 20036. 1988. (This appealing book uses a minimum of words to show the push and pull of forces on a building.)

Thanks For Your Support!

Challenge: Build a structure that will support 400 grams at least 25 cm above the base.

Design Team

Height of structure

_____

Amount of mass supported

_____

cream.

Hint: To test your structure, start with an empty container and slowly increase the mass. Strengthen your structure as needed.

Draw your structure.

BRIDGE IT

Topic
Bridges

Key Question
Challenge: Build a straw bridge that spans a 30 cm gap and supports ____ grams on its road bed.

Focus
Students will work as a team to meet the challenge of building a straw bridge to certain specifications.

Guiding Documents
Project 2061 Benchmarks
- *Scientific laws, engineering principles, properties of materials, and construction techniques must be taken into account in designing engineering solutions to problems. Other factors, such as cost, safety, appearance, environmental impact, and what will happen if the solution fails also must be considered.*
- *Even a good design may fail. Sometimes steps can be taken ahead of time to reduce the likelihood of failure, but it cannot be entirely eliminated.*

NRC Standards
- *Identify a simple problem.*
- *Propose a solution.*
- *Implementing proposed solutions.*
- *Evaluate a product or design.*
- *Communicate a problem, design, and solution.*

NCTM Standards
- *Develop spatial sense*
- *Make and use measurements in problems and everyday situations*

Math
Geometry and spatial sense
Measurement
    linear
    mass
Counting

Science
Physical science
    force

Technology
Engineering
    structures

Integrated Processes
Observing
Collecting and recording data
Comparing and contrasting
Applying

Materials
For each group:
    30 plastic drinking straws, minimum
    material to join straws (see *Management 2*)
    beverage, fruit, vegetable, or soup can (see *Management 4*)
    meter stick, meter tape, or metric rulers
    scissors

For the class:
    balance
    gram masses

Background Information
Of the many kinds of bridges in the world, the truss bridge seems a logical choice when constructing with straws. Truss bridges use triangles for structural support. The triangular braces add strength to a structure. Experience with this concept, gained in *Working Out the Wiggles* and *Straws Take a Stand*, can and should be applied to this bridge-building task.

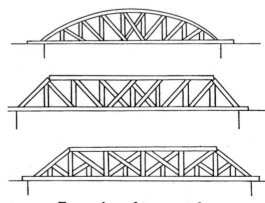

Examples of truss styles

The practical purpose for a bridge is to allow people or various forms of transportation to cross a gap. The road bed is the part of the bridge on which cars, trains, etc. actually travel. The bridge's ability to support mass on the road bed must be proven and is the place it is tested in this activity.

Aside from the engineering aspects, much of the value of this activity lies in challenging students' problem-solving skills and creativity along with developing cooperation and perseverance.

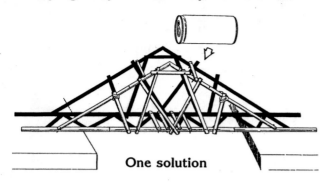

One solution

Management

1. *Working Out the Wiggles* and *Straws Take a Stand* are highly recommended preliminary activities.
2. A combination of methods will likely be needed to connect the straws in this activity. Choose from the options suggested in *Constructing With Straws* (see *Table of Contents*) and assemble the appropriate materials.
3. Students should work in groups of two or three.
4. Measure the mass of several canned products from your pantry and decide on one whose mass falls somewhere between 300 and 500 grams. (The milliliters stated on cans cannot be equated with grams of mass.) All groups should use cans with the same mass. Your decision will then determine the number to be written in the *Challenge*. For example, if you are using soda cans with a mass of 380 grams, you might write "370" in the blank. The goal should be slightly less than the actual mass used for testing. The reason for this is to provide a cushion for slight variations in mass, even among the same cans.

    To test a minimum, you can't go under the amount and it is hard to be equal to the amount, so it is better to be slightly over the amount. Food processors add a little extra amount of food to their packages so the total mass will not fall below the minimum stated on the label.

    The opposite can also be true. If a bridge sign says, "2-ton limit", you would expect it can hold slightly more than that. The engineers will have allowed for a little extra weight.
5. The bridge should rest on two flat desks or tables but not be attached to them in any way. It might be called a "free-sitting" bridge.
6. Encourage students to sketch a preliminary design on the back of the paper before beginning.
7. To help students keep track of the number of straws they use, you may wish to set up a check-out system. They could record the number they receive at the beginning and each time they get more. When the project is completed, they can subtract the straws they didn't use from the total number of straws checked out.

Procedure

1. Present the *Challenge*. Distribute the activity page and building materials. Explain various methods of joining straws if they do not have previous experience with them.
2. Instruct each student group to build their bridge across a 30-cm span between two desks or tables. The bridge cannot be attached to the desks.
3. Describe how to test the strength of the bridge without making it collapse. Have students carefully place the can on its side in the center of the road bed. They should not immediately let go of the can but slowly let the bridge take more of its mass. If they feel the bridge giving way, students should lift the can up, strengthen the bridge, and test again until the can rests on it without being held.
4. Let the groups begin construction.
5. Have each group complete the construction report and sketch their bridge.
6. Guide students on a room tour of the completed bridges and hold a concluding discussion.

Discussion

1. How did you decide where to start? Did you draw a design first? Did you talk it over? Or did you just start and see what would happen?
2. What problems did you have in meeting the challenge? What did you do about them?
3. What do you like about your bridge?
4. How many triangles does your bridge have?
5. How does your bridge compare with others? (Awards might be given for the most unusual bridge, the bridge built with the least amount of straws, the most pleasing bridge, the safest bridge, etc.)

Curriculum Correlation
Resources

Use the following books to explore the variety of bridge designs with students. Which bridges could be made with straws? What other materials could be used for model bridges?

Carter, Polly. *The Bridge Book*. Simon & Schuster. New York. 1992. (A historical look at the development of bridges, with emphasis on invention and the problem-solving process, delivered through cartoons and text.)

Robbins, Ken. *Bridges*. Dial Books. New York. 1991. (Beautifully written text with uniquely-colored drawings based on actual photographs of bridges in northeastern United States.)

Wilson, Forrest. *Bridges Go From Here To There*. The Preservation Press, National Trust for Historic Preservation, 1785 Massachusetts Avenue, N.W., Washington, D.C. 20036. 1993. (Clever black-and-white illustrations show the push and pull of forces on various kinds of bridges. Minimal words.)

BRIDGE IT

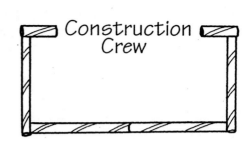

Construction Crew

Challenge: Build a straw bridge that spans a 30 cm gap and supports _____ grams on its road bed.

Construction Report

Methods used to join straws:

_____

_____

_____ # of straws used
_____ total length of bridge
_____ width of bridge
_____ mass supported

Sketch your bridge.

Student-Made Measuring Tools

It is well worth the time for students to make their own measuring tools. Handmade tools tend to be well cared for because students feel ownership of them. Instructions for making these tools follow.

Paper meter tapes

Linear Measure

Goal: 2 per student, each a different color

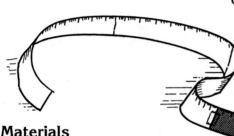

Duplicate the meter tape page on different colors of copy paper. Give two different colors to each student. Have students cut out the strips and glue or tape like colors together. For durability, laminate the paper tapes.

The meter tapes can be used singly for activities measuring short distances. To measure long distances, have students combine alternately-colored meter tapes to create a visually easy-to-read measure even at a distance.

Materials
2 or more colors of copy paper
Scissors
Glue or tape

String meter measure

Goal: 1 per group

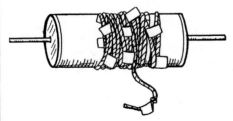

Materials
30-50 m of string
Masking tape
Meter tape
Permanent marker
Scissors
Potato chip can or
    1 lb. coffee can
Dowel, optional

Make a knot a few centimeters from one end of the string; this represents zero. Use a meter tape to mark the one-meter point on the string with the permanent marker. (Both the tape and the string must be taut.) Continue this process until the entire string is marked at one-meter intervals. To make tabs, fold 5-cm pieces of masking tape in half around the string, positioning them right before or after each meter mark. Label the tabs, beginning with "0 m" at the knot. Starting with the higher-numbered end, wrap the string around a can to keep it from tangling. To easily wrap and unwrap the string, insert a dowel through both ends of the can.

To measure distances to the nearest meter, one student should hold the zero end of the string while another holds the dowel and unwinds the string. If greater accuracy is desired, a single meter tape can be used together with the string measure. For example, if the length of a tree's shadow is between 24 and 25 meters, a meter tape can be placed along the 24-meter mark of the string, allowing measurement to the nearest centimeter.

Balance

Goal: 1 per group

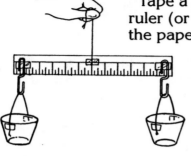

Materials
Ruler
70 cm of string
2 plastic cups
2 paper clips
Tape
Scissors

Tape a 20-cm piece of string to the top center of the ruler (or thread through the center hole and tie.) Open the paper clips and tape or hang them on the two ends of the ruler so that the hooks hang below the bottom of the ruler. Tape a 30-cm piece of string to each cup and hang the cups on the paper clips. If the ruler does not balance evenly, add pieces of clay or tape small objects to the side that is high or reposition the top center string to the right or left.

Non-customary masses

Materials
Use objects with uniform mass such as plastic bears or tiles.

Customary masses

Goal: 1 set per group (10 g, 20 g, 50 g, 100 g)

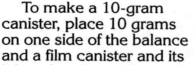

Materials for uniform masses
4 empty film canisters
   (free at most stores that do
   their own photo developing)
Salt, sand, or BBs
Permanent marker
5-minute epoxy glue, optional
Colored gummed labels,
   optional
Gram masses or centicubes

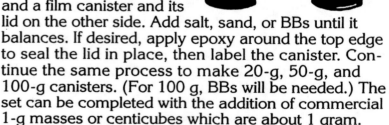

To make a 10-gram canister, place 10 grams on one side of the balance and a film canister and its lid on the other side. Add salt, sand, or BBs until it balances. If desired, apply epoxy around the top edge to seal the lid in place, then label the canister. Continue the same process to make 20-g, 50-g, and 100-g canisters. (For 100 g, BBs will be needed.) The set can be completed with the addition of commercial 1-g masses or centicubes which are about 1 gram.

   If colored labels are used to color-code mass sets, the labels should be placed on the canister before determining mass.

Materials for non-uniform masses
Rocks, bolts, blocks of wood,
   old locks, etc.

Measure and label the mass of non-uniform objects. These objects then become measuring tools. For example, it might take a 57-gram rock, a 91-gram block of wood and 8 small paper clips (4 grams) to balance a pair of scissors.

Measuring Volume

Goal: 1 set per group
(small, medium, and large jars)

Materials
Small, medium, and large
    straight-sided jars
Permanent marker
Graduated cylinder or a large
    syringe (found in pet stores),
    marked in milliliters

Have students use the graduated cylinder or syringe to measure an amount of water equal to the increment chosen for each jar. Small jars would most likely be calibrated in 10-milliliter increments, larger jars in 25-, 50-, or 100-ml increments. Pour the water into the jar, and carefully mark the level of the water and label the unit on the side of the jar. Repeat this process until you have filled the jar.

Individual or group sets can be stored in shoe boxes, one of several ways to organize and manage these measuring tools.

— adapted from *Student Made Measuring Tools*
by Dave Youngs

Rulers Line Up

Topic
Linear measurement

Key Question
How can you divide a strip for measuring into ten equal units?

Focus
Students will become familiar with "deci" units. They will also see the need for using customary units of measure rather than non-customary units.

Guiding Documents
Project 2061 Benchmark
- *When people care about what is being counted or measured, it is important for them to say what the units are (three degrees Fahrenheit is different from three centimeters; three miles from three miles per hour).*

NRC Standard
- *Tools help scientists make better observations, measurements, and equipment for investigations. They help scientists see, measure, and do things that they could not otherwise see, measure, and do.*

NCTM Standard
- *Develop the process of measuring and concepts related to units of measurement*

Math
Linear measurement
  deci-

Integrated Processes
Observing
Comparing and contrasting
Collecting and recording data
Interpreting data
Generalizing

Materials
Construction paper
Lined paper
Overhead transparencies

Background Information
This activity provides students with the opportunity to measure many different objects using a non-customary

unit. They will divide their unit into 10 equal parts to gain practice in measuring deci-units. The multiple measuring experiences done here can later be transferred to the use of meter and decimeter measures.

At the conclusion of this activity, students should discover that their non-customary units are not well known to others. This fact makes communication of their measures difficult; therefore, they should begin to see the need to use customary units when trying to communicate the length of objects to others.

Management
1. Cut various lengths of construction paper strips for students to use as measuring devices. Make each strip about 2.5 cm (1 inch) wide and between 15-30 cm (6-12 inches) in length. Each student should have his or her own measuring strip which will be called a roo.
2. The method of dividing the paper strips into 10 equal-sized parts requires a good deal of problem-solving skills—especially with the longer strips. Allow students the time to grapple with finding a solution.
3. Students will need ruled notebook or tablet paper.
4. To help facilitate the procedure for calibrating the measuring strip, make a transparency of a ruled sheet of paper or draw equally spaced lines on the transparency film. Cut your own measuring strip from another sheet of transparency film—a colored transparency adds good contrast.
5. When the lined-paper method is used to calibrate the rulers, those students with longer strips of paper may have difficulties. Encourage them to seek suggestions from other students. Some strategies they may discover are: two sheets of lined paper can be taped together; every other line can be numbered to spread out the scale.
6. Prior to this activity, students should have had multiple experiences using non-customary units of linear measurement such as: footsteps, hand spans, pencil lengths, paper clip lengths, etc.

Procedure
1. Distribute construction paper strips, one to each student. Inform the students that these strips, roos, will be the rulers with which they will measure several different objects.

$\boxed{}$ = 1 roo

2. Invite the students to find something in the classroom that is one roo long. Have them record the object and its length, using the name of their unit.

3. Allow time for students to find and record things on *Chart A* that measure two, three, and five roos. If necessary, remind them to label their measures.

4. Ask the students to find something that is one-half a roo. After the students have located the objects, have them share their strategies for "knowing" how to determine one-half a ruler length.

5. Inform the students that you want them to be able to measure in tenths. Ask them how they could equally divide their rulers into 10 equal parts. (Many will say to fold it in half, in half again, and in half once more before they discover that this strategy will not work for finding tenths.) Elicit a variety of strategies, allowing time to try them.

6. Tell the students that you are going to share a method that will help them divide their rulers into equal parts. Place the lined transparency on the overhead projector. Ask the students how many parts they need in order to divide their rulers into tenths. [10] Turn the lined transparency so that the lines run vertically. Demonstrate for the students how to number the lines from zero to 10.

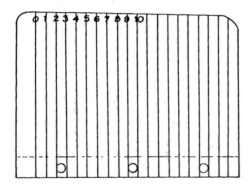

7. Take the transparent ruler and place the upper left corner on the zero line. (The ruler will be longer than the 10 numbered lines.) Ask the students what they should do since the ruler won't fit between the zero and the 10. (If say to cut it off, tell them that they can't alter the length of their ruler.)

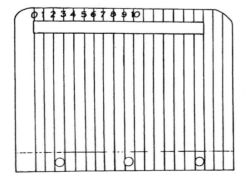

8. Demonstrate to the students how to hold the upper left corner of the ruler on the zero line and to pivot the ruler until the upper right corner is on the 10 line. (It may help to have students highlight line 10.)

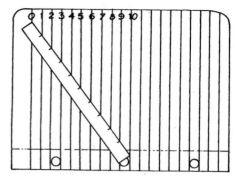

9. Show them how to make little marks where the lines on the transparency intersect the top edge of their ruler.

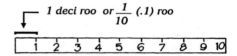

1 deci roo or $\frac{1}{10}$ (.1) roo

10. Once all marks are in place, have the students number the marks.

11. Tell them that "deci" is the prefix for tenth, so if something is three deci-roos in length, they would need to measure to the three-tenth's mark.

12. Now have the students find objects in the room for the measures listed in *Chart B*.

13. Finally, ask students to record the measure of the objects listed in *Chart C* to the nearest deci-roo.

Discussion

1. How does your roo compare with the person's next to you?

2. Is it important that each of your deci-roos be the same size? Explain.

3. Why is it important to label our measures?

4. Compare the length of your pencil using your roo with the length another person determines for that same pencil using their roo. Are they same or different? Explain any differences in the measure.

5. What do you think the reaction of a clerk at a home improvement store would be if you called and asked for a certain measure of lumber using your roo units? How could this type of problem (using units which are not well known) be avoided? [Use units which are well known such as meters and feet.]

6. What other problems are there with using roos? [Our measured lengths aren't the same because our roos aren't the same length.]

7. Deci means one-tenth so you divided your ruler into ten equal parts. Centi is the prefix that means

one-one hundredth. What do you think you would have to do to your ruler in order to measure centi-units? [divide it into 100 equal-sized parts] How could you do that? [Each of the one-tenth parts needs to be marked into 10 equal-sized parts.] Does it seem reasonable to use the lined paper? Explain. [No, because the lines are too far apart. We would probably just have to estimate the one hundredths.] (Note: Prefixes for the metric system which end in the letter i, such as deci—1/10, centi—1/100, and milli—1/1000, are all fractional parts of the metric unit.)

Extensions
1. If students are able, have them record their measures in units using decimals, fractions, and deci-units. For example: 2.4 roos, 2 4/10 roos, 24 deci-roos.
2. Have students use the lined paper to divide their measuring strips into other fractional parts such as fourths, eighths, etc.
3. Have students approximate the centi-roos on their rulers. Have them measure and record to the nearest centi-roo.
4. Do *Metric Scavenger Hunt* from the AIMS publication *Math + Science, A Solution.*

Curriculum Correlation
Literature
Myller, Rolf. *How Big is a Foot?* Dell Publishing. 1990.

Rulers Line Up

Chart A

Object	Length
	1 _roo_
	2 ___
	3 ___
	5 ___
	$\frac{1}{2}$ ___

Chart B

Object	Length
	1 deci _roo_
	2 deci ___
	3 deci ___
	5 deci ___
	$\frac{4}{10}$ deci ___
	$\frac{6}{10}$ deci ___
	$\frac{11}{10}$ deci ___
	$\frac{17}{10}$ deci ___
	$\frac{35}{10}$ deci ___

Chart C

Object	Length
Your pencil	
This paper	
A shoelace	
Height of door jam	
Hair	

Links to Length

Topic
Measuring meters

Key Question
How long a paper chain can you make from one piece of paper?

Focus
Students are challenged to create the longest paper chain possible from limited materials and then measure the results.

Guiding Documents
Project 2061 Benchmarks
- *Length can be thought of as unit lengths joined together, area as a collection of unit squares, and volume as a set of unit cubes.*
- *Spreading data out on a number line helps to see what the extremes are, where they pile up, and where the gaps are. A summary of data includes where the middle is and how much spread is around it.*

NRC Standards
- *Plan and conduct a simple investigation.*
- *Employ simple equipment and tools to gather data and extend the senses.*
- *Communicate investigations and explanations*

NCTM Standards
- *Develop the process of measuring and concepts related to units of measurement*
- *Construct, read, and interpret displays of data*

Math
Measurement
    linear
Estimation
    rounding
Problem solving
Graphing
Statistics
    range, mode

Integrated Processes
Observing
Collecting and recording data
Comparing and contrasting
Controlling variables

Materials
For each group of two:
    scratch paper
    one 12"x18" piece of construction paper
    glue or transparent tape
    scissors

For the class:
    meter tapes, sticks, or string
    construction paper strips (see *Management 6*)
    2-3 meters of roving yarn
    20 small paper squares

Background Information
Students are challenged to make the longest paper chain possible from one piece of paper. Those students who plan carefully by identifying the factors which will influence the results will likely make longer chains. One factor is the width of the paper strips. The narrower the strips, the more loops can be made. Another factor is the amount of overlap used when taping or gluing the loops. The most efficient and length-extending method is to bring the ends of the strips together and tape them where they meet. If glue is used, some overlap is necessary. The length of the paper strips is a third factor. Longer strips mean fewer loops and less length lost due to overlap or the intertwining of the loops.

A line plot, in the form of paper loops, is used to graphically organize and represent data in this activity. This technique was developed in the late 1970's by a statistician named J.W. Tukey. From a line plot, we can find the most frequent values and see the overall distribution of the results in much the same way as is portrayed in a bar graph. It is another tool for organizing and presenting data.

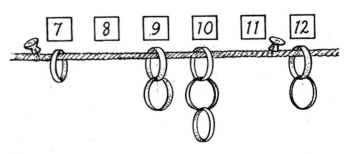

Management
1. Planning, actual construction, and measuring the chain may be spread over two or more days.

2. Students should be paired. Working with a partner allows the sharing of ideas during planning and also speeds the completion of the chain.
3. Use a variety of construction paper colors.
4. A series of colorful student-made meter tapes are ideal for seeing the meter as a repeated unit when measuring the paper chains. One long tape can be used for all measurements. Find directions in *Student-Made Measuring Tools* (see *Table of Contents.*)
5. Rules you may wish to consider using:
   a. A paper chain is defined as a series of complete loops or links. All of each paper strip must form a single loop.
   b. Tape cannot be used to extend loops. The strips of paper must either meet or overlap each other.
   c. Chains must be sturdy enough to be stretched and not break during measuring. Decide whether students will be allowed to flatten loops in half to extend their length.
6. Prepare the class line plot (graph). A variety of materials could be used. Yarn and paper squares are one suggestion. String the yarn parallel to the floor and at a height where it is visible and accessible to students, perhaps along a bulletin board or chalkboard. Attach the paper squares at even intervals. They will become the meter labels once the range has been determined. Cut paper strips, about 9"x 3/4", one for each pair of students.
7. The finished chains may be used to create a colorful room sculpture. Try intertwining chains as well as stringing them along the walls and hanging them from the ceiling.

Procedure
1. Ask the *Key Question*. Give student pairs scratch paper and tape or glue with which to experiment. Allow sufficient time for students to test strategies using the scratch paper and develop a plan of action.
2. Distribute the activity sheet and have students record their plan.
3. Give each pair the piece of construction paper and have them construct a chain.
4. Instruct students to measure the length of their chain. They can round to the nearest meter or centimeter and record the results as, for example, 10 m, 37 cm or 10.37 meters.
5. Bring the class together and ask them how the range for the class could be found. (They might suggest taking a quick poll.) Finding the range will determine the numbering for the line plot. For example, if no chain is longer than 20 meters, the paper squares could be numbered 1 to 20. If the shortest is 8 m and the longest 25 m, the numbering might begin at 7 and stop at 26.
6. Give each group a paper strip and have them form a loop around the yarn and under the number

showing the length of their chain rounded to the nearest meter. If more than one group has the same length, their loops should be attached to the preceding loops in a chain-like fashion. (See the illustration in *Background Information.*)
7. Direct students to record the class line plot on their activity sheet by numbering the line and drawing the loops.
8. Have students identify the range and mode. Hold a concluding discussion.

Discussion
1. What things did you think about when you were making your plans? [the width of the paper strips, the length of the strips, the amount of overlap or how to make the loop without wasting length, etc.]
2. Share your plan.
3. What plan was the most successful? What was good about the plan?
4. If you were to try this again, what would you do differently?
5. If you had a 15-sheet package of the same-sized paper you used today, would your chain go around the perimeter of your classroom? How many times? Would your chain cover the length of a football field? (A football field is 110 meters from end zone to end zone or 91 meters from goal line to goal line.)

Links to Length

Partners _____

How long a paper chain can you make from one piece of paper?

Plan:

Length of finished chain:

CLASS RESULTS

Length in Meters

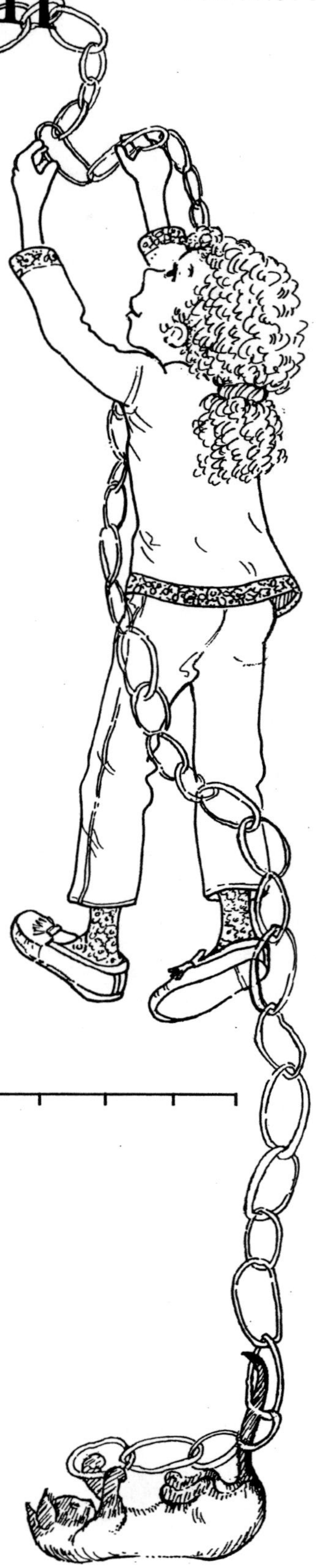

Class range _____

Most common distance (mode) _____

Are You A Square?

Topic
Linear measurement/human body

Key Question
How does your height compare with your arm span?

Focus
Each student will discover how their height and arm span compare. Students will also examine and interpret class data.

Guiding Documents
Project 2061 Benchmarks
- *Measuring instruments can be used to gather accurate information for making scientific comparisons of objects and events and for designing and constructing things that will work properly.*
- *Measurements are always likely to give slightly different numbers, even if what is being measured stays the same.*

NRC Standards
- *Employ simple equipment and tools to gather data and extend the senses.*
- *Communicate investigations and explanations*

NCTM Standards
- *Make and use measurements in problems and everyday situations*
- *Construct, read, and interpret displays of data*

Math
Estimation
Measurement
   length
Bar graph

Science
Life science
   human body

Integrated Processes
Observing
Collecting and recording data
Comparing and contrasting
Classifying
Interpreting data

Materials
Meter sticks or tapes (see *Management* 2)
3-column class bar graph (see *Management* 1)
Transparency of *Class Results* page
Sticky notes, 3 colors
Adding machine tape

Background Information
Measurement is an important means of obtaining data. As students measure each other, then double-check those measurements, they should begin to realize that measurements are never exactly the same even though the same thing is being measured. Some discrepancy may be due to careless measuring, but it is also due to the very nature of measurement. Measurement is always an estimation because the increments can always be divided into smaller units. Measuring to the nearest half centimeter is more precise than to the nearest centimeter. Measuring to the nearest millimeter is more precise than to the nearest half centimeter. A millimeter can be divided into still smaller segments.

Because measurement is never exact, it becomes rather clear that a "square" should not just be defined as someone who measures *exactly* the same number of centimeters in height as in arm span. The challenge is to arrive at an acceptable range for the definition of a square.

Several fairly consistent ratios can be found by measuring the human body: circumference to height, femur to height, etc. In the big picture, the height and the arm span for human beings are nearly the same. Of course there are exceptions to this generalization. A key to your results will be in how a square is defined. Two examples from the world of athletics are:
- Shawn Bradley of the NBA has a height of 7 feet, 6 inches and an arm span of 7 feet, 6 inches.
- Michael Gross, the West German Olympic gold medal swimmer of the 1980's, is 6 feet, 7 inches tall and has an arm span of 7 feet, 4 5/8 inches. (A definite exception to the rule!)

Management
1. Prepare a 3-column class bar graph, labeling the columns *square*, *tall rectangle*, and *far-reaching*

rectangle. Use a different color sticky note for each body type. Make a matching color key.

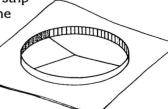

Square	Tall Rectangle	Far-reaching Rectangle

2. For each measuring area, tape two meter sticks end-to-end vertically to measure height. Also tape two horizontally at an average student's shoulder height to measure arm span. Set up at least two measuring areas.

3. Use groups of three with two students measuring the third one. Height measurement should be taken with shoes off. Place a ruler at the top of the head and parallel to the floor to read the measurement more accurately. The arm span measurement should be taken with the back against the wall and arms outstretched along the meter sticks at shoulder height. Measure from fingertip to fingertip.

4. Allow 45 minutes or more for this activity.

5. To illustrate how a bar graph can be turned into a circle graph, remove the sticky notes and attach them, edge to edge, to a strip of adding machine tape. Placing a piece of paper (at least 24" square) under it, pull the paper strip into a circle. Trace the circle and draw a radius at each place where a new color of sticky notes begins.

Procedure

1. Ask the *Key Question* and give students the activity sheet.

2. Have students predict and record their height and arm span.

3. Determine whether to round measurements to the nearest millimeter, half centimeter, or centimeter. Discuss how to measure accurately (see *Management 3*).

4. Have groups of three measure each other's height and arm span. They should check their results by measuring more than one time.

5. After recording their measurements, students should complete the L-shaped bar graph and record their height and arm span on the *Class Results* transparency.

6. Put the transparency on the overhead projector. Ask questions such as:
   a. What do you notice?
   b. Who has the greatest difference?
   c. Which students are square?
   d. How much wiggle room (margin for error) do

we need? How will we define a square—exactly the same measurements, up to 1 cm difference, up to 2 cm difference? Why? [possible errors in measurement, rounding process]
   e. What does providing wiggle room do to our results? Do we now have more or less squares than at first?

7. Have students compare their results to the three illustrations and record whether they are a square, tall rectangle, or far-reaching rectangle. Using the data on the transparency, have the class also decide whether each person is a square, tall, rectangle, or far-reaching rectangle.

8. Instruct students to place a colored sticky note in the correct column of the class bar graph.

9. Discuss the results. Follow up by showing them how the data can be illustrated with a circle graph (see *Management 5*).

Discussion

1. Should we round our measurements to the nearest centimeter, half centimeter, or millimeter? (Centimeters are easier to measure, but there will be less variation in the results. Millimeters are harder to measure, but give more precise results.)

2. How close should the measurements be to make a square? (1- or 2-centimeter range)

3. Which shape is most common? Which is most rare?

4. Do you have a twin?

5. Do you think age has anything to do with the results? Explain why you think that way?

6. Would another class have the same results? (see *Extension*)

7. What new questions do you have?

Extension

Measure another class or adults at school. Record and compare.

Curriculum Correlation
Language Arts

Write to athletes, actors, etc. and ask them for their height and arm span.

Home Link

Have students measure their family. Does the same shape run in the family?

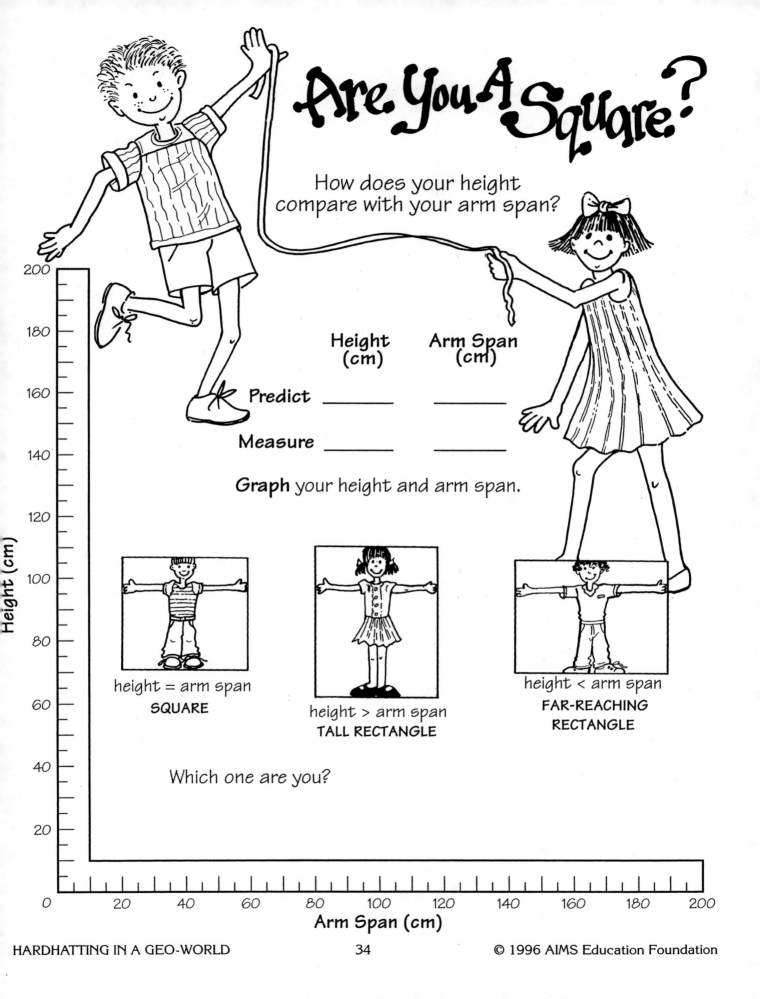

Are You A Square?

How does your height compare with your arm span?

	Height (cm)	Arm Span (cm)
Predict	_____	_____
Measure	_____	_____

Graph your height and arm span.

height = arm span
SQUARE

height > arm span
TALL RECTANGLE

height < arm span
FAR-REACHING RECTANGLE

Which one are you?

Height (cm) *(y-axis: 20 40 60 80 100 120 140 160 180 200)*

Arm Span (cm) *(x-axis: 0 20 40 60 80 100 120 140 160 180 200)*

34

Are You A Square?

CLASS RESULTS

Name	Height	Arm Span	SQUARE	TALL RECTANGLE	FAR-REACHING RECTANGLE
1.					
2.					
3.					
4.					
5.					
6.					
7.					
8.					
9.					
10.					
11.					
12.					
13.					
14.					
15.					
16.					
17.					
18.					
19.					
20.					
21.					
22.					
23.					
24.					
25.					
26.					
27.					
28.					
29.					
30.					
31.					
32.					

HARDHATTING IN A GEO-WORLD   35   © 1996 AIMS Education Foundation

BEAR FACTS

Topic
Linear measurement

Key Question
How do you compare to your bear?

Focus
Students will use teddy bears to measure and compare with their bodies.

Guiding Documents
Project 2061 Benchmarks
- *Measuring instruments can be used to gather accurate information for making scientific comparisons of objects and events and for designing and constructing things that will work properly.*
- *Add, subtract, multiply, and divide whole numbers mentally, on paper, and with a calculator.*

NRC Standard
- *Employ simple equipment and tools to gather data and extend the senses.*

NCTM Standards
- *Select and use computation techniques appropriate to specific problems and determine whether the results are reasonable*
- *Make and use measurements in problems and everyday situations*

Math
Counting
Estimation
Measurement
    linear
Whole number computation
    subtraction

Integrated Processes
Observing
Collecting and recording data
Comparing and contrasting

Materials
Teddy bears (see *Management 1*)
Metric measuring tapes (see *Management 2*)

Background Information
This activity provides an appealing context for students to practice linear measurement skills, measuring both straight lengths as well as *around* objects.

Management
1. Before doing the activity, ask students to bring a well-loved teddy bear from home. You may wish to have an extra teddy bear available for students who have no bear and wish to adopt one for the day. Or students may work in pairs and share a bear.
2. In preparation for measuring, have students color, cut out, and assemble the measuring tape found in the back of this book. To measure student height, vertically attach two measuring tapes to the wall.
3. Students need to work in pairs to measure each other. This works nicely, too, if they are sharing a bear.
4. Be sensitive toward students reluctant to take tummy measurements. Maybe one of the partners could volunteer to provide this data for both.

Procedure
1. Arrange ahead of time for a "bring your bear to school" day.
2. Have students record the bear's name and picture on the first activity sheet.
3. Discuss how each measurement will be done. Height should be taken without shoes. Arm length is defined as the shoulder joint to the finger tip, running along the outer part of the arm. Leg length extends from the hip joint (bend a leg to find it) to the sole of the foot, along the outer part of the leg. The tummy should be measured where a belt would be worn.
4. Instruct students to measure themselves and their bears with the tape and record this data in the table.
5. Have students compare measurements by finding the differences.
6. Discuss the results (see *Discussion 1-3*). Have students express their height in "bears" and describe one way that their bear is special.
7. Distribute the second activity sheet and tell each student to draw a picture of themselves and a picture of their bear.
8. Have students compare characteristics beyond size by asking, "How are you like your bear?" "How are you different from your bear?" Instruct students to tell, write, or draw at least three responses to each question.

Discussion
1. How much taller are you than your bear?
2. How many bears tall are you?
3. Which measurement—height, arm, leg, or tummy—is closest to being the same as the bear?
4. In what other ways can we compare ourselves to our bears?

Extensions
1. Arrange bears in a line or a train from small to tall or light to dark....etc.
2. Make a collection of bear facts for a class Big Book that tells about bears at school.
3. Take photographs of students and their bears for a scrapbook.
4. Choose one bear and measure each child's height in bears. Make a bear graph of the results.

BEAR FACTS

Owner _____

Bear's Name

Snapshot

How do you compare to your teddy bear?

ME:
BEAR:
Difference:

	Height (cm)	Arm Length (cm)	Leg Length (cm)	Around Tummy (cm)

How many bears tall are you?

What makes your bear special?

BEAR FACTS

How **do** you compare to a bear?

ME

BEAR

How are you **like** your bear?

How are you **different** from your bear?

Cups 'n' Stuff

Topic
Measuring mass

Key Question
If volume is equal, how does the mass compare?

Focus
The mass of five different materials with equal volume will be measured and ordered by students.

Guiding Documents
Project 2061 Benchmarks
- *When people care about what is being counted or measured, it is important for them to say what the units are (three degrees Fahrenheit is different from three centimeters, three miles from three miles per hour).*
- *Use numerical data in describing and comparing objects and events.*

NRC Standards
- *Objects have many observable properties, including size, weight, shape, color, temperature, and the ability to react with other substances. Those properties can be measured using tools, such as rulers, balances, and thermometers.*
- *Tools help scientists make better observations, measurements, and equipment for investigations. They help scientists see, measure, and do things that they could not otherwise see, measure, and do.*

NCTM Standards
- *Apply estimation in working with quantities, measurement, computation, and problem solving*
- *Understand the attributes of length, capacity, weight, mass, area, volume, time, temperature, and angle*
- *Develop the process of measuring and concepts related to units of measurement*

Math
Measurement
    mass, customary
    volume, non-customary
Ordering
Estimation
    rounding
Graphing

Integrated Processes
Observing
Collecting and recording data
Comparing and contrasting
Controlling variables
Drawing conclusions

Materials
For each group:
    1/2 cup each of five different materials (see *Management* 2)
    5 small plastic cups, about 3 oz. each
    balance
    gram masses
    glue
    crayons or colored pencils

Background Information
The intent of this activity is to give students experience in determining mass. If some of the materials have nearly the same mass, students may also realize that using a balance to measure is a more accurate way of comparing than by lifting the cups.

The underlying reason for the differences in mass is the varying densities of the materials. Students at this level are not yet ready to formally deal with density but they are given an experience which will lead to the presentation of that concept when they are developmentally ready.

Management
1. Organize the class into groups of four or five. The groups should work together but each group member will benefit by completing an activity sheet.
2. Each group will need about 1/2 cup or 125 ml each of five different materials. Food suggestions: pinto or navy beans, popcorn kernels, rice, salt or sugar, barley, macaroni, lentils, cereal, cornmeal, etc. Other suggestions: sand, vermiculite, pet food, dirt, etc.
3. It is helpful to have students fill the cups for their group earlier in the day. Schedule the rotation so the measuring area will not be crowded. To control volume, cups of the same size should be filled to the brim with each material and leveled by sliding an index card across the top.

Procedure
1. Have each group retrieve their filled cups. Review the fact that they have measured equal volumes of five different materials. Then ask the *Key Question*.

2. Explain that each group will order the materials from heaviest to lightest by two methods, lifting and measuring. For students who have difficulty finding a systematic strategy for lifting the cups, suggest the following method:
   a. Compare all five cups by lifting two at a time, one in each hand. Find the heaviest and the lightest and place them on a flat surface about a ruler's length apart. Each group member should have a turn lifting the cups and then the group should agree on order placement.
   b. Compare the three that are left. Find the heaviest and the lightest and place them in the appropriate order between the other two cups.
   c. Ask, "Where does the one that is left belong?"
3. To record the order obtained by lifting, have students glue a few pieces of the material in each of the cups on the activity sheet.
4. Direct groups to gather a balance and gram masses, then measure and record the mass of each cup of material. You may wish to have students include an estimate of mass as well as actual mass.

Material	Estimated Mass	Actual Mass

5. Have students graph the results in order from heaviest to lightest. Remind them to label the graph and give it a title.
6. To record their measuring order in another way, instruct students to glue a sample of each material in the second set of cups on the activity sheet.
7. Revisit the *Key Question* as you discuss the results.

Discussion
1. How did your lifting results compare with your measuring results? [Lifting is less accurate than measuring so, for materials with nearly the same mass, there may be differences in order.]
2. Use greater than and less than to write several inequalities about the materials. (Example: macaroni < salt)
3. What is your conclusion about mass when volume is equal? [It is likely mass will not be equal.]
4. We measured different kinds of solid materials in this activity. What else could we measure in the same way? [liquids] What do you predict about the results?
5. Make a plan to test the mass of liquids with the same volume. (Students will need to find a solution for potential spilling problems. One solution: Use one cup as the volume measurer, drawing a line somewhere *below* the brim. Measure each liquid up to this line, then pour it into another cup. Rinse and dry before each new liquid is measured.)

Extension
Do the activity again using liquids, as designed by students in response to *Discussion 5*.

Cups 'n' Stuff

If volume is equal, how does the mass compare?

heaviest | BY LIFTING | lightest

heaviest | BY MEASURING | lightest

Measure and record the mass of each material.

Put in order from heaviest to lightest on the graph.

Peddle the Metal

Topic
Measuring mass

Key Question
How much money do I need in order to buy your jewelry collection?

Focus
Students will make pasta jewelry and determine the selling price by measuring the number of grams of each piece.

Guiding Documents
Project 2061 Benchmarks
- *When people care about what is being counted or measured, it is important for them to say what the units are (three degrees Fahrenheit is different from three centimeters, three miles from three miles per hour).*
- *Judge whether measurements and computations of quantities such as length, area, volume, weight, or time are reasonable in a familiar context by comparing them to typical values.*

NRC Standard
- *Objects have many observable properties, including size, weight, shape, color, temperature, and the ability to react with other substances. Those properties can be measured using tools, such as rulers, balances, and thermometers.*

NCTM Standards
- *Make and use measurements in problems and everyday situations*
- *Select and use computation techniques appropriate to specific problems and determine whether the results are reasonable*

Math
Measurement
    mass
Money
Whole number operations
    multiplication

Integrated Processes
Observing
Collecting and recording data
Comparing and contrasting
Applying

Materials
String
Scissors
Pasta (see *Management*)
Balances
Gram masses
Calculators
Paper for price tags and display

Background Information
Many items we buy are priced per unit measure. At the grocery store, fresh fruit and vegetables as well as meat are sold by the pound. Medication, in the form of pills, is labeled by number of milligrams. Gold is a commodity that is also priced this way; in some markets, even gold jewelry is sold by the gram.

Students have the opportunity to simulate the practice of pricing according to mass through a combination art project/measuring experience. In addition to challenging their creativity, they are able to apply gram measurement in a realistic way. They also work with our money system and must determine whether the prices they calculated are reasonable for the numbers used.

Management
1. Divide the class into groups of four or five.
2. Gather three or more kinds of pasta that can be strung such as salad macaroni, elbow macaroni, and mostaccioli.
3. To make colored pasta simulating beads or emeralds, rubies, and sapphires, pour about 1/4 c. rubbing alcohol and several drops of food coloring into a jar with a lid. Add the pasta, close the jar, and shake to coat. Spread the pasta on several layers of newspaper to dry.
4. Determine the cost per gram based on the ability level of your students. The simplest approach is to set the cost in whole dollars (such as $3 per gram.) If you want students to deal with decimals, choose a cost below one dollar (such as $.85) for easier computation, or above one dollar (such as $4.70) for more challenging computation. Another option is to check the newspaper in order to use the current price of gold. (One ounce of gold equals 28 grams.)
5. Have the materials available in a designated area. One or two members from each group can gather what they need.

6. You can control the activity in one of three ways: a) limit the time for creating the jewelry, b) limit the number of jewelry pieces that can be made, or c) limit the number of grams of pasta used by each group, say 100 grams. (For this last option, use the *Challenge* shown on the easel on the activity sheet in place of the *Key Question*.)

Procedure

1. Tell students that each group will be designing and displaying a jewelry collection. They can make matching sets of jewelry or individual pieces. Explain that jewelry is sometimes priced by the number of grams it measures. The cost of their jewelry will be set at _____ per gram.
2. Distribute the activity page and have students write the cost per gram.
3. Have one or two persons from each group gather some starting supplies of string and pasta. Instruct the groups to make their jewelry collections.
4. Direct each group to get a balance and gram masses. Have them find and record the mass of each piece of jewelry on the activity sheet, then compute its price according to the cost set per gram.

Example

Jewelry	Mass	Price (at $3 per gram)
necklace 1	16 g	$48.00
necklace 2	22 g	$66.00
bracelet	7 g	$21.00

5. Have groups set up a jewelry display complete with price tags including the number of grams.
6. Organize a way for the groups to go window shopping among the displays.
7. Discuss the results.

Discussion

1. How many things can you think of that are sold by mass or weight? (fresh fruits and vegetables, pills, gold jewelry, etc.)
2. How did you know your price calculations were correct? (Students should explain their reasoning for why their answers made sense. For example, if 16 grams were calculated at $.85 per gram and the answer was $18, students should reason that because $.85 is below one dollar and there are 16 grams, the answer has to be less than $16. For the same problem, if they obtained an answer of $136, they should reason that it could not possibly be that much and question whether they put the decimal in the right place. Correct answer: $13.60)
3. Is your jewelry collection designed for wealthy people, people without very much money, or is there something for every pocketbook?

4. Which one or two pieces of your collection do you consider the most unique?

Extensions

1. Students who are wearing jewelry might find the cost of their pieces using the same cost-per-gram as in the activity.
2. Have students figure the price of their jewelry based on the current price of gold. Gold prices are reported by the ounce. One ounce equals 28 grams.
3. Expand the activity into a consumer simulation by having students actually buy and sell their jewelry using play money. They could record their total sales for the day. Optional: include the current sales taxes.
4. For older students, determine a "cost per hour" for labor. Have them calculate the cost of the gold used to make their jewelry and add on the labor cost to determine the selling price. You may also want to attach a percentage value for profit.

Peddle the Metal

Design and make a collection of jewelry to be sold at_____ a gram.

Record the mass and price of each piece.

Make a window display of your jewelry showing number of grams and price.

Filling Stations

Topic
Measuring capacity/volume

Key Question
How much will these containers hold?

Focus
Students will compare the capacity of various containers.

Guiding Documents
Project 2061 Benchmarks
- *Mathematical ideas can be represented concretely, graphically, and symbolically.*
- *When people care about what is being counted or measured, it is important for them to say what the units are (three degrees Fahrenheit is different from three centimeters, three miles from three miles per hour).*
- *Tables and graphs can show how values of one quantity are related to values of another.*

NRC Standard
- *Tools help scientists make better observations, measurements, and equipment for investigations. They help scientists see, measure, and do things that they could not otherwise see, measure, and do.*

NCTM Standards
- *Understand the attributes of length, capacity, weight, mass, area, volume, time, temperature, and angle*
- *Make and use measurements in problems and everyday situations*
- *Construct, read, and interpret displays of data*

Math
Measurement
    capacity/volume
Graphing

Integrated Processes
Observing
Predicting
Collecting and recording data
Comparing and contrasting

Materials
For each group:
    5 different containers (see *Management 2*)
    graduated cylinders
    bucket or plastic tub
    scissors
    12"x18" construction paper
    transparent tape or glue

Background Information
Both *volume* and *capacity* are measures of three-dimensional spaces. Volume is the amount of **space occupied** by an object or a material in an object. Capacity is the amount of **available space** in an object, how much it holds. In this activity, we are comparing the capacity of various containers by using a graduated cylinder to measure the volume of water each one holds.

A graduated cylinder is generally labeled in milliliters. It takes 1,000 milliliters to make one liter. The liter, a basic unit of volume measurement, is defined as 1,000th of a cubic meter. It is a little larger than a quart.

Students often have limited experience with three-dimensional measurement, yet it has many useful applications including cooking, buying gasoline, taking cough syrup and other liquid medicines, and checking the amount of milk or soda in a beverage container. This activity is one means of expanding their measurement skills.

Management
1. Divide the class into groups of four or five. Although students will work in groups, consider having each student complete an activity sheet and graph.
2. Gather containers of similar size but of different shapes, heights, and widths such as tomato paste cans, tomato sauce cans, tuna cans, cups and jars of various sizes, 1/2 pint milk cartons, etc.
3. For the containers suggested in *Management 2*, 100-, 250-, and 500-milliliter graduated cylinders will be useful. The 100-ml graduated cylinder can be used to obtain more precise readings. If larger containers are used, a 1,000-ml graduated cylinder may be needed.
4. When measuring with a graduated cylinder, set it on a flat surface and read at eye level. Because the water is attracted to the sides of the graduated cylinder, it will form a concave shape. Remind students to read the water level at the bottom of the meniscus, near the center of the water line.

read here

          © 1996 AIMS Education Foundation

5. Each group will need a large water container such as a five-gallon plastic bucket (check the cafeteria) or a plastic tub. Not only will it hold the group's water supply but students will pour and measure over the container to help contain spills.
6. For the cylinders on the graph, either have students use their lined writing paper or make copies, preferably on colored paper, of the lined page included in this activity. Cut the copies in half along the dotted line. They will need enough to make five cylinders.
7. If possible, do this activity outdoors or in a place where water spills are not a problem. A few towels may be needed for mopping spills.

Procedure

1. Have the class assemble into groups. Display one set of containers, introduce the *Key Question*, and distribute the activity page.
2. Instruct students to draw the five containers on their page. The containers may be labeled by description such as "tomato paste" or with letters such as A, B, C, D, and E.
3. Direct groups to write the predicted order of the containers from largest capacity to smallest capacity, using the labels on their drawings.
4. Have each group take their water supply, graduated cylinders, and containers to the designated area. Instruct them to fill each container to the brim with water and carefully pour it into a large graduated cylinder. This should be done over their bucket or tub. For more precise readings, they can then transfer smaller quantities to a 100-milliliter graduated cylinder. A record should be made, either next to their drawings on the activity sheet or on a piece of scratch paper.
5. Oversee the clean-up of the workspace and equipment and have students return to the classroom.
6. Distribute the construction paper and lined paper for the graph.
7. Have students determine the numbering of the graph based on their highest milliliter reading and number each of the five lined papers in the same way. Tell them to cut along the line marked zero.

[graph image with lines and measurements]
400
350
300
250
200
150
100
50
0

8. For each graph cylinder, direct students to use a straight edge to mark the number of milliliters

measured for a container, cut along the mark, roll it into a cylinder (overlapping so lines meet), and tape or glue.
9. Tell students to attach the cylinders to the construction paper, in order from largest capacity to smallest capacity, to form a graph like that shown on the activity page. Either label or tape/glue the picture drawn of the container under each cylinder.

Discussion

1. Why is it important to set the graduated cylinder on a table top before reading the water level? [It prevents the water from being tipped which causes inaccurate readings.]
2. The results of which container most surprised you?
3. How close were your predictions to your results?
4. How much would a container hold if you had to use the entire lined section of your paper?
5. What did you most enjoy about this activity?

Extensions

1. Find a simple recipe and have students use metric measures to make the food.
2. Do the related activity, *All Bottled Up*, found in the AIMS publication *Water, Precious Water*.

Home Link

1. Have students check the liquid measuring cup in their kitchens at home. Most now have two scales, cups and milliliters. About how many milliliters are in one cup?
2. Encourage students to look in their pantries for food containers labeled with number of milliliters. They might record the products and number of milliliters and share this data with the class. What kinds of products are labeled in milliliters?

Filling Stations

Filling Stations

Filling Stations

Pleased as Punch

Topic
Measuring volume

Key Question
Which punch looks and tastes best?

Focus
Students will plan various mixes of punch, measure according to their recipes, and give their opinion of the results.

Guiding Documents
Project 2061 Benchmarks
- *When people care about what is being counted or measured, it is important for them to say what the units are (three degrees Fahrenheit is different from three centimeters, three miles from three miles per hour).*
- *Tables and graphs can show how values of one quantity are related to values of another.*
- *Measure and mix dry and liquid materials (in the kitchen, garage, or laboratory) in prescribed amounts, exercising reasonable safety.*

NRC Standard
- *Employ simple equipment and tools to gather data and extend the senses.*

NCTM Standards
- *Understand the attributes of length, capacity, weight, mass, area, volume, time, temperature, and angle*
- *Make and use measurements in problems and everyday situations*

Math
Measurement
   volume
Graphing

Integrated Processes
Observing
Collecting and recording data
Comparing and contrasting
Controlling variables

Materials
For the class:
   3-6 kinds of powdered drink mix (see *Management 2*)
   3-6 pitchers

For each group:
   about 15 transparent cups, 6 oz. or more
   100 ml graduated cylinder
   crayons or colored pencils

Background Information
Volume is a measure of three-dimensional regions. It is the amount of space occupied by an object or a material in an object. In this activity, students use graduated cylinders to measure the volume of each kind of punch that is part of their recipes.

The graduated cylinder is generally labeled in milliliters. One thousand milliliters make one liter, a little more than a quart.

Volume measurement is often less familiar to students than linear, mass, and other forms of measurement. Its practical applications extend from cooking and baking to the buying of gasoline to the labeling of beverages such as milk and soda. Through measuring experience, such as that provided in this activity, students can build their understanding of volume.

Management
1. Have students work in groups of four or five.
2. When purchasing the powdered drink mix, choose flavors with vivid coloring such as grape, cherry, strawberry, orange, and lime. Make the drink mixture ahead of time and have it available in pitchers before beginning the activity.
3. Be mindful of students who are diabetic or for some other reason are not suppose to ingest sugar.
4. Consider doing this activity outdoors, as spills are probable. Have paper towels handy.
5. Caution students not to plan all the recipes at one time because the results of one may led to a different kind of mix to try.
6. Graduated cylinders should be washed with soap and water before and after this activity.
7. Each group will need one cup for each drink mix flavor (labeled with the flavor), one cup for each

of their recipes (labeled A, B, C, and D), and one taste-testing cup for each group member (labeled with each person's name.)

Procedure
1. "Today you have the chance to create a new punch by mixing any combination of the individual punches I have made. Your challenge is to find a combination that looks and tastes the best."
2. Distribute the activity sheet and explain that each group first needs to make a recipe or plan. To do this, they should color the *Recipe A* graduated cylinder to represent the mix of punches and amounts they want to use, in increments of ten and making a total of 100 milliliters. If necessary, they should create a key. It is helpful to write the amounts to be measured next to each color.

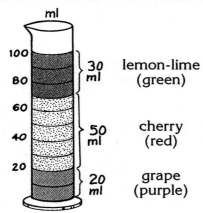

Example

3. Have each group gather a graduated cylinder, eight to eleven transparent cups, and a labeled cup of each kind of punch in the designated area. Have students label four cups A, B, C, and D. The remaining cups will be used for taste tests. Each student should label one cup with his/her name.
4. To avoid over- and under-measuring errors, students should measure one kind of punch at a time, following their recipe. Using the above example, they would first pour 20 ml of grape punch into the graduated cylinder, adding or pouring back a little until they get the right amount. When the amount is correct, it should be poured into the transparent cup labeled A. Next, they should measure 50 ml of cherry punch and add it to cup A, followed by 30 ml of lemon-lime punch.
5. Instruct each group to use their activity sheet to draw or describe the punch they created.
6. Have students follow the same procedure for *Recipe B*, then *Recipe C*, and finally *Recipe D*.
7. Direct each group to conduct a taste test and declare their winning recipe (A, B, C, or D). Have them give their punch an interesting name.

Discussion
1. What problems, if any, did you have mixing the punch?
2. What, to your group, is a good-looking punch?
3. How did your group come to agree on the winning punch?
4. Look at your winning punch recipe. Order the flavors from least to greatest amount.
5. Compare the recipes of other groups. Can you find some that are similar to yours? What recipes did other groups have that you would like to try?

Extension
Have students make a simple recipe using metric measurements.

Curriculum Correlation
Art
Have students design a packet for their favorite punch.

Language Arts
Have students write an advertisement for their favorite punch. They can include a jingle or a song. Let the students make a video of themselves performing the advertisement.

Minute Minders

Topic
Time: one minute

Key Question
How reliable are your one-minute time keepers?

Focus
Students will perform various tasks for one minute, then repeat the tasks the same number of times to test their reliability as time keepers.

Guiding Documents
Project 2061 Benchmarks
- *Keep records of their investigations and observations and not change the records later.*
- *Offer reasons for their findings and consider reasons suggested by others.*
- *Use numerical data in describing and comparing objects and events.*

NRC Standard
- *Employ simple equipment and tools to gather data and exend the senses.*

NCTM Standards
- *Develop the process of measuring and concepts related to units of measurement*
- *Collect, organize, and describe data*

Math
Measurement
   time
Counting

Integrated Processes
Observing
Estimating
Collecting and recording data
Comparing and contrasting
Drawing conclusions

Materials
Clock or other time-piece with a second hand
Ball which bounces
Scratch paper

Background Information
The purpose for this activity is to help students become aware of the length of a minute as well as to realize the need for measuring time based on an even rate.

Students will find that the tasks performed are not altogether reliable as time keepers. One of the reasons is that variables are not controlled. Sometimes a ball bounces higher, sometimes lower. Your hand might get tired as you write your name continually. Jumping jacks may not be done at an even rate. You can decrease or increase the number of breaths you take a minute. Even if a conscious effort were made to control variables, there would be discrepancies. It is not easy for a person to control the variations with which they write their name or bounce a ball. This points to the need for a consistent measure of time, clocks and watches. The tasks are interesting, though, as an approximation of a minute.

It is tempting for students to manipulate or change the results in order to reach their estimate or to have their second timing match one minute. This is a good opportunity to point out that a scientist's goal is to find the truth. Fudging the facts will not give you the truth.

Management
1. Students should work with a partner.
2. Students are given four repetitious tasks to perform. You may want to devise a short list of possibilities from which students will choose the fifth task. It should require little equipment and be able to be performed by an individual as opposed to a team.
3. Students will first be timed estimating when a minute has passed. Then they will be timed twice during each task, once while performing the task for one minute and then while duplicating the previous number of repetitions of the task.
4. The tasks may be done in any order. In fact, you may want to organize pairs so some start with bouncing a ball outside while others are writing their name inside. Caution: They should count breaths either before doing tasks involving exercise or after they are sufficiently recovered from them.
5. Emphasize that this is not a competition with others in the class. If it were, variables would have to be controlled. Instead, the purpose is for students to gain a sense of the length of a minute.

Procedure
Preliminary timing
1. "How long is a minute? Explain that each person will have a chance to guess when a minute has passed. Pair students and have one of each pair face away from the clock. Give an audible "start" and have the person facing away from the clock tell their partner when they think a minute has passed by softly saying, "Stop" or "Now." The partner can then tell them how many seconds have passed.

2. Have the partners trade places and repeat, with the other partner estimating when a minute has passed. "Who estimated less than a minute? Who estimated more than a minute? How close were you?"

First timing of task
3. Give students the activity sheet and explain the procedure, Have students choose and write the fifth task in the blank.
4. Instruct students to estimate how many times they can do the first task. Their partner should then time them, giving soft, audible "start" and "stop" signals. Emphasize that they should make an honest effort at the task and not try to match their estimate.
5. Have partners switch roles, with the one who just finished performing the task now becoming the timer.

Second timing of task
6. Inform students that they will again perform the same task. This time the performer will use his/her previous results to try to determine when one minute has elapsed while facing away from the clock. (If a name was written 17 times in a minute the first time, the name should again be written 17 times.)
7. The partner should give the "start" signal. The person doing the task should count his/her repetitions and say "stop" when the number needed is reached. The partner will then tell how much time elapsed.
8. Repeat *Step 4* through *Step 7* for each task.
9. Bring the class back together to discuss and draw conclusions raised by the *Key Question*, "How reliable are your one-minute time keepers?"

Discussion
1. How did the time of your second trial compare with one minute?
2. How reliable are these activities as time keepers? [They are alright for estimating time but not reliable as a more precise measure of time.] Why do you think this is so? [It is difficult to perform activities at an even rate.]

3. What surprised you about the results?
4. What did you learn about a minute?
5. When would it be important not to waste minutes? [when you have a time limit to finish something such as taking a test or doing chores, when you're in a race at a track meet, when you must finish your homework before you can play, when you're getting ready for a party or to go to a movie, etc.)

Curriculum Correlation
Language Arts
1. Neasi, Barbara. *A Minute is a Minute.* Children's Press. Chicago. 1988. (A picture book with a simple poem about how the length of minute doesn't change but sometimes seems longer or shorter depending on what we are doing. Very appropriate for sparking discussion with intermediate students. Currently out-of-print, but check libraries, etc. for a copy.)
2. Have students explore the meaning of folk sayings and idiomatic expressions about time. They might also illustrate the sayings as does Fred Gwynne in *A Chocolate Moose for Dinner* and *The King Who Rained,* both published in 1988 by Simon and Schuster, Books for Young Readers. Some examples:
> A stitch in time saves nine.
> Lost time is never found again.
> Time flies when you're having fun.
> Time waits for no man.
> In the nick of time
> Time on your hands
> Killing time
> The time of your life
> From time to time
> Behind time
> Big time
> Give a hard time
> In less than no time
> In a minute
> Once upon a time

Minute Minders

Estimate how many times you can do each activity in one minute. Try it and record the results. Repeat each activity the number of times you counted and have your partner time how long it takes.

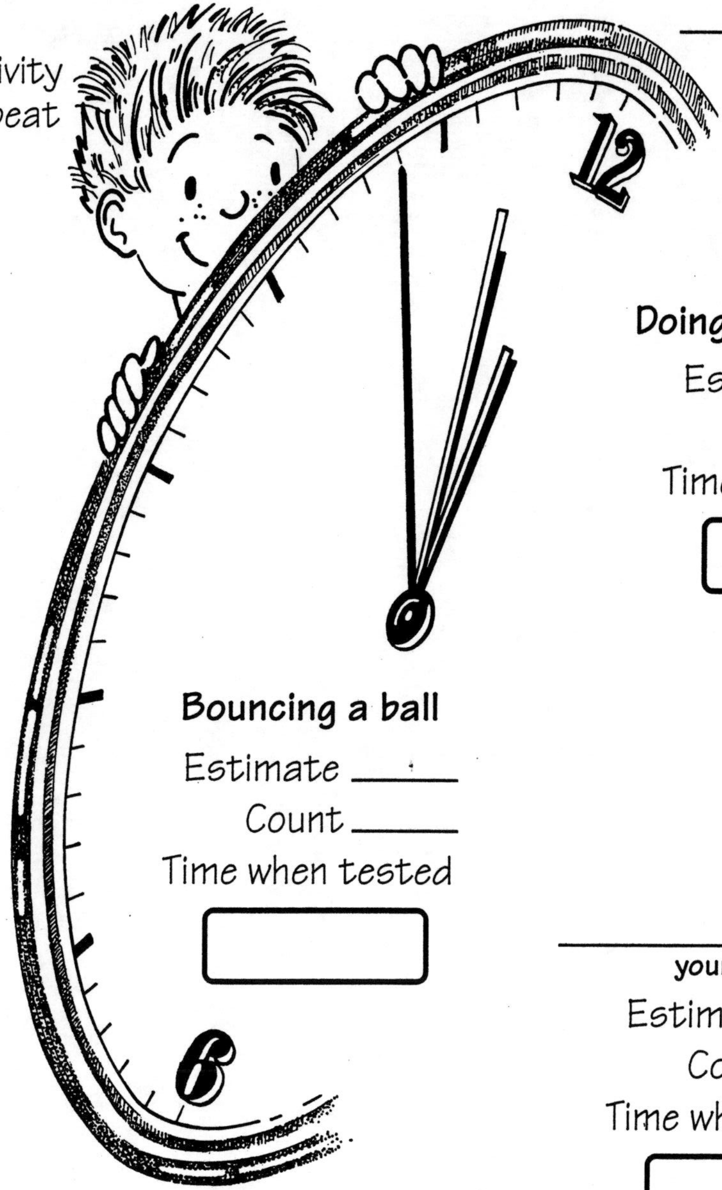

Partners _____

Doing jumping jacks
Estimate _____
Count _____
Time when tested _____

your choice _____
Estimate _____
Count _____
Time when tested _____

Bouncing a ball
Estimate _____
Count _____
Time when tested _____

Writing your name
Estimate _____
Count _____
Time when tested _____

Taking breaths
Estimate _____
Count _____
Time when tested _____

How good are these activities as time keepers?

From Wedges to Wangles

Topic
Non-customary angle measurement

Key Question
How many wangles fit in these angles?

Focus
Students will construct and use three-dimensional wedges (wangles) to measure angles found in nature and in objects made by people.

Guiding Documents
Project 2061 Benchmarks
- *Mathematical ideas can be represented concretely, graphically, and symbolically.*
- *Numbers and shapes—and operations on them—help to describe and predict things about the world around us.*
- *Use numerical data in describing and comparing objects and events.*

NRC Standard
- *Employ simple equipment and tools to gather data and extend the senses.*

NCTM Standards
- *Recognize and appreciate geometry in their world*
- *Understand the attributes of length, capacity, weight, mass, area, volume, time, temperature, and angle*
- *Develop the process of measuring and concepts related to units of measurement*

Math
Measurement
 angles
Geometry and spatial sense

Integrated Processes
Observing
Grouping
Collecting and
 recording data
Comparing and
 contrasting

Materials
For each group:
 transparent tape
 scissors
 12 craft sticks
 white glue
 12"x18" piece of construction paper

Background Information
Angles are found outdoors, indoors, almost everywhere we look. They are an integral part of many two-dimensional and three-dimensional shapes we encounter, from the painted lines of a basketball court to the silhouette of jagged mountains.

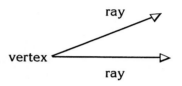

An angle is made of two rays with a common endpoint (vertex). The measure of an angle can be taken by subdividing it into uniform wedge-shaped units. This is a very different kind of measurement than the linear scale on a ruler, a thermometer, or a graduated cylinder frequently used by students. Just as the centimeter is a repeated unit in length measurement, the wedge is a repeated unit in angle measurement. Since the wedge is an unfamiliar unit of measurement, students need multiple experiences using it. This will give them a foundation for understanding protractors and, eventually, more advanced mathematics.

The three-dimensional wedge-shaped unit that is used in this activity has been named a wangle. Because folding will not be exact, a certain amount of approximation will take place when the pictures are measured.

Management
1. Organize the class into groups of two.
2. Each group will need to make 12 wangles. Copy the wangle patterns on colored paper if possible.
3. Consider making wangles and measuring the pictures on one day, then making the craft stick measurers and grouping angles on another day. The wangles will need to be saved for the second day.

Procedure
Part 1
1. "You have had experience with measuring in meters, grams, degrees Celsius, etc. But there is a very different kind of measurement that we are going to explore today. Instead of reading a scale

like we do on a ruler or a thermometer, we are going find into how many wangles (wedge-shaped units) an angle can be divided." (If necessary, review the terms *ray* and *vertex*.)

2. Distribute the wangle patterns. Instruct students to cut them out, fold along the broken lines, and tape at the vertex.

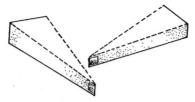

3. Distribute the three pages of pictures. Direct students to use their wangles to measure the angles formed by the bold lines (rays). Have them record the number of wangles by each picture.

Part 2
4. Give each group the craft sticks, glue, and the last activity page. Have them use their wangles to make the stick measures listed on the page.

5. When the glue is dry, instruct students to use their stick wangles to find the number of wangles in each of the angles on the page. Inform students that these are how angles are drawn for geometry. They should record the number inside each angle.

6. Explain that they are now going to search through the three picture pages and the last activity page to find matching sets of angles. Have students cut out the angles and angle pictures that match.

7. Distribute a large piece of colored construction paper and direct students to glue the sets of angles in groups on the paper, then label them by number of wangles.

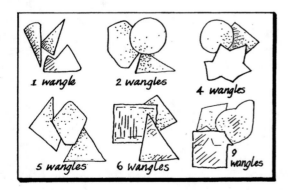

Angle groups
    1 wangle: shell, ladder, angle C
    2 wangles: ferris wheel, gazelle, angle D
    4 wangles: snowflake, maple leaf, angle B
    5 wangles: tree, slide, angle A
    6 wangles: sailboat, bookcase, angle F
    9 wangles: roof, chair, angle E

8. Encourage students to find objects inside and outside the classroom that fit their various stick wangles.

Discussion
1. How many wangles fit in each picture?
2. Look at each of the pictures again. What other angles in them could be measured?
3. There are angles all around us. What are some that you have found and measured?
4. How many wangles wide would the door have to be open in order to walk in or out?

Extension
Cut, order, and glue the remaining angle pictures from smallest to largest.

Curriculum Correlation
Art
Draw a real-world object incorporating a specific angle such as those on the picture pages.

From Wedges to Wangles

From **Wedges** to **Wangles**

How many wangles?

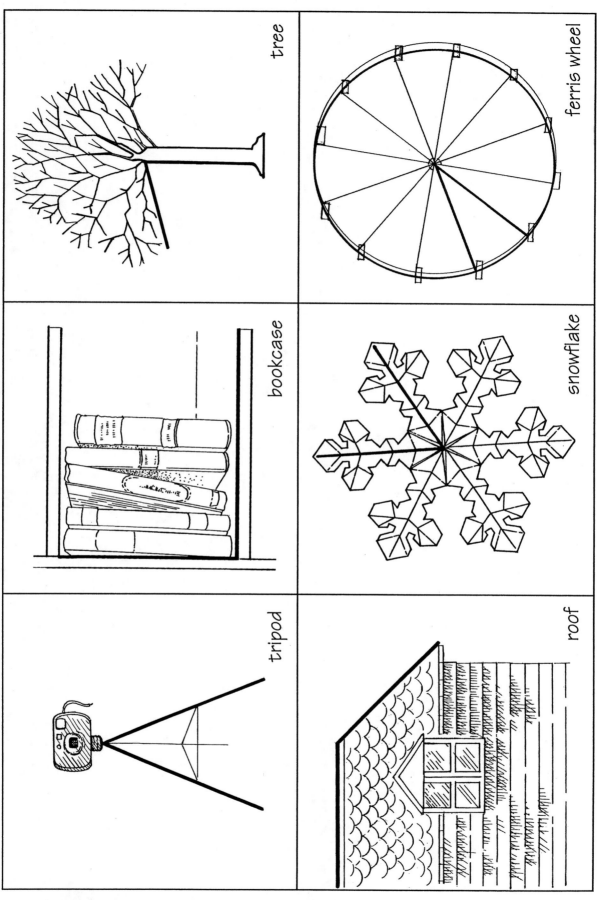

tree

ferris wheel

bookcase

snowflake

tripod

roof

From Wedges to Wangles

How many wangles?

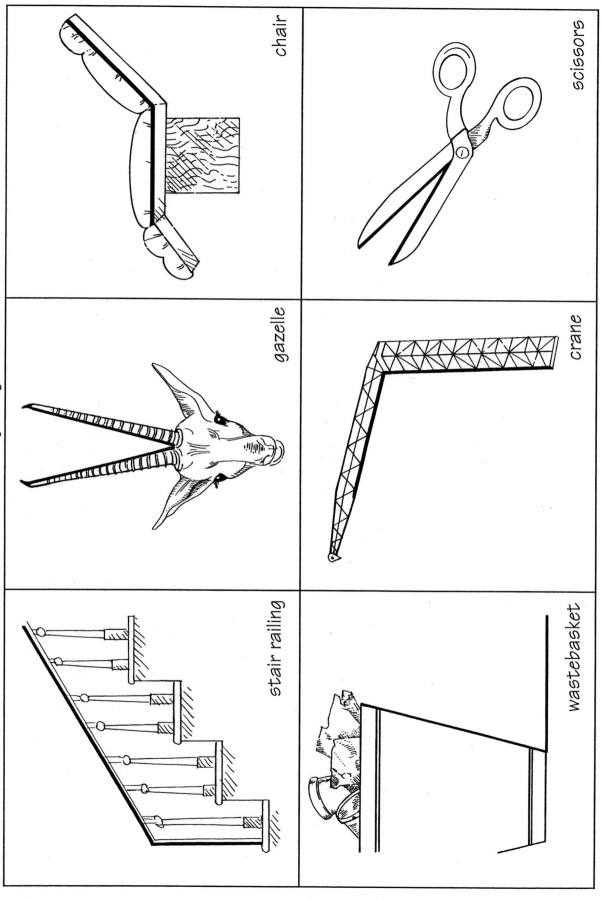

chair

scissors

gazelle

crane

stair railing

wastebasket

From Wedges to Wangles

How many wangles?

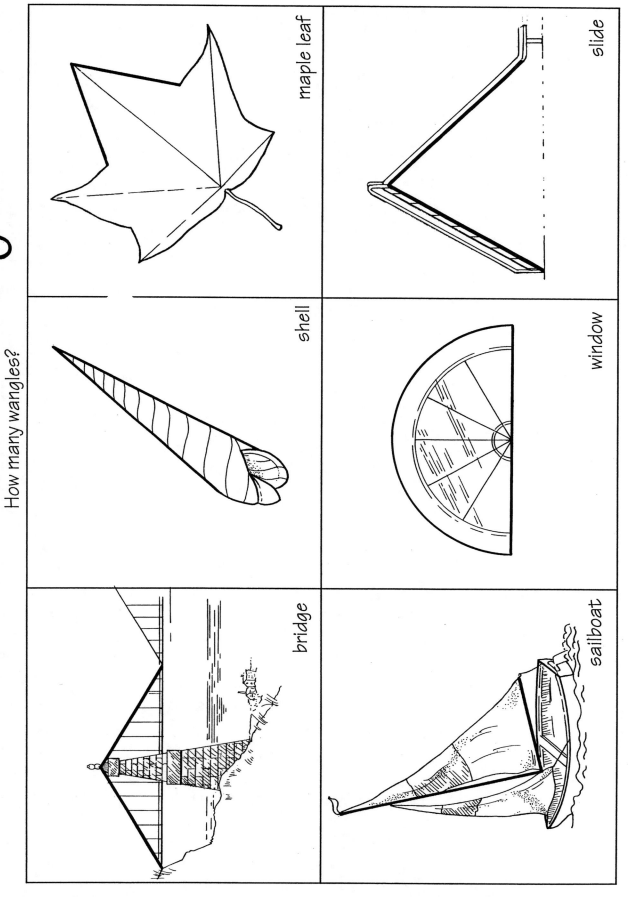

maple leaf

slide

shell

window

bridge

sailboat

60

From Wedges to Wangles

Use your wangles to make stick measures of 1, 2, 4, 5, 6 and 9 wangles. Label your stick measures on both sides.

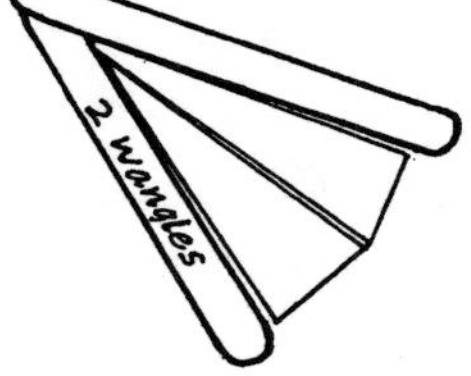

Record the angle measures inside each of these angles. Match these angles to those pictured on the previous pages. Cut and glue groups of matching angles onto a piece of construction paper.

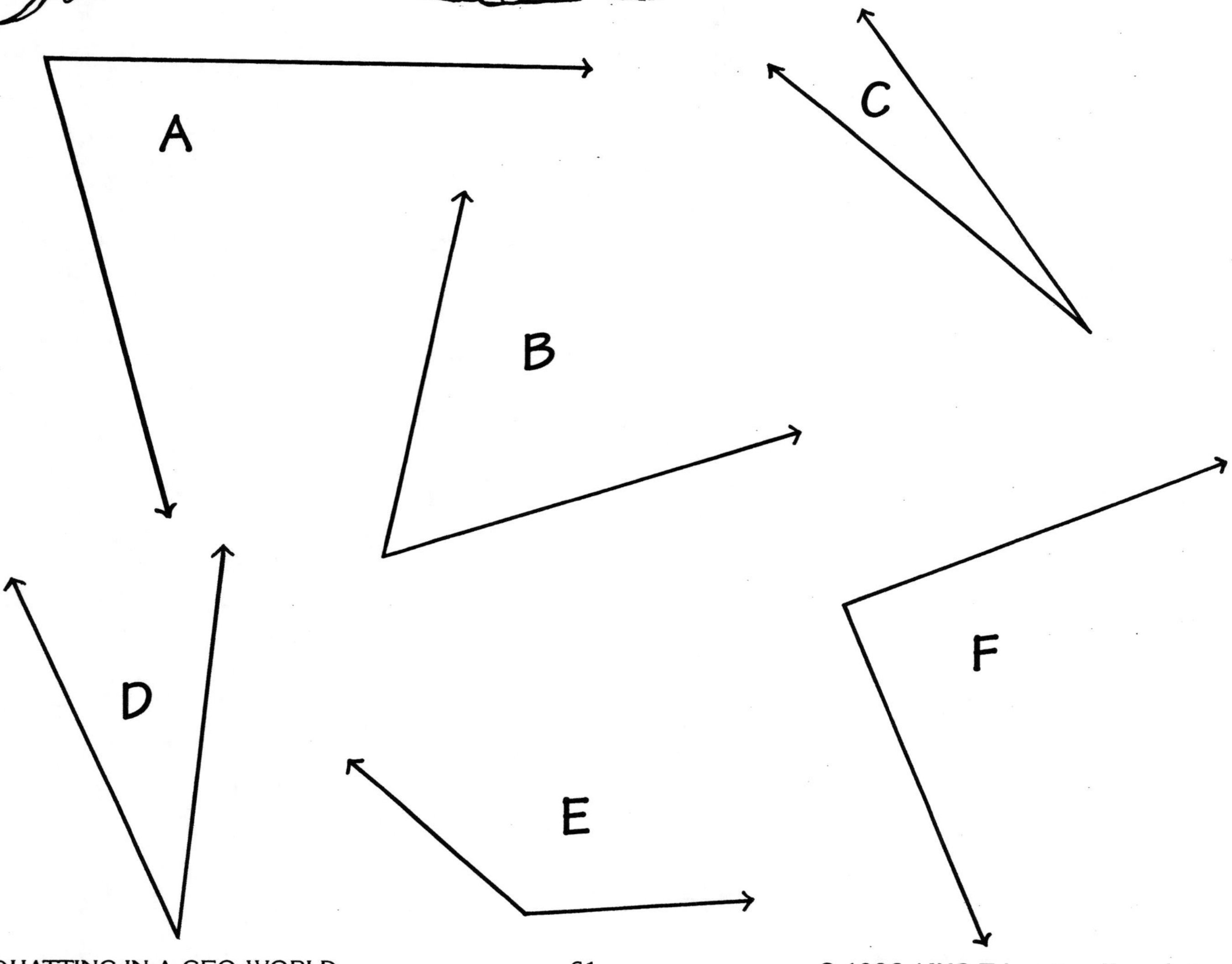

A

B

C

D

E

F

Waxed Wangles

Topic
Non-customary angle measurement

Key Question
How can we make a tool to measure angles?

Focus
Students will fold a non-customary protractor and use it to construct a clock and measure angles formed by the clock's hands.

Guiding Documents
Project 2061 Benchmarks
- *Measuring instruments can be used to gather accurate information for making scientific comparisons of objects and events and for designing and constructing things that will work properly.*
- *Make sketches to aid in explaining procedures or ideas.*
- *Use numerical data in describing and comparing objects and events.*

NRC Standard
- *Employ simple equipment and tools to gather data and extend the senses.*

NCTM Standards
- *Understand the attributes of length, capacity, weight, mass, area, volume, time, temperature, and angle*
- *Develop the process of measuring and concepts related to units of measurement*
- *Relate geometric ideas to number and measurement ideas*

Math
Measurement
   angles
Geometry and spatial sense
Problem solving

Integrated Processes
Observing
Collecting and recording data
Comparing and contrasting
Applying

Materials
For each student:
   waxed paper, about 6" square
   scissors
   tagboard, about 2"x4"
   1 paper fastener

Background Information
This activity continues the exploration of angle measure begun in *From Wedges to Wangles*. An angle can be measured by counting the number of uniform wedge-shaped units into which it can be divided. We have named the wedge-shaped unit used in this activity a wangle, an invented word. After working with individual wangles, students should progress to using a tool that measures multiple wangles. We are always looking for easier ways to do mathematics and measuring tools provide a means toward this goal.

Learning to use the wangle protractor is another step in building conceptual understanding of angle measurement and eventually will lead to the use of the traditional protractor which measures in degrees.

Management
1. To build the concept of angle measurement, experience with *From Wedges to Wangles* should precede this activity.
2. When showing times on the clock, remind students the clock hands must be in the same position as a real clock. For example, they can't put the minute hand on the six and the hour hand on the one because that position would not normally occur on a real clock.

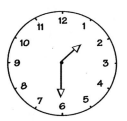

legal   not legal

3. Choose times that are appropriate for your students. Younger students may work with hours only, older students with half hours and the matching angle exploration suggested in *Procedure 8*.
4. One angle is formed by the various clock hand positions but it can be measured in two ways. Tell students to take the small measure for this activity.

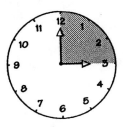

3:00
small measure

3:00
large measure

Procedure

1. Inform students that a tool called a protractor is used to measure angles. They will be making a wangle protractor and use it to explore the geometry of clocks. Explain that angles can be measured by dividing them into wedge-shaped units. The wedge-shaped unit they will be using is called a wangle, an invented word.

2. Distribute the first activity sheet and waxed paper to each student. Have them cut out the wangle template.

3. Guide students through the folding process shown on the sheet.

4. Introduce the challenge of making a clock by asking, "How can we use our wangle protractor to mark the hours on a clock?" Have students explain their thinking as they respond with suggestions. You may want them to solve this problem in small groups rather than as a class. (They should conclude that the clock is divided into 12 sections and the protractor into 24, so every two wangles equals one hour.)

5. As students mark their clocks, distribute the tagboard and paper fasteners. Explain that they will use the tagboard to cut two clock hands of different lengths and attach them to the clock with the paper fastener.

6. Give students the second activity sheet while they cut out the clock.

7. Name a time and have students show it on their clocks. Direct them to use the wangle protractor to count the number of wangles in the angle formed by the clock hands. Have them record the data by drawing the clock hands, shading the angle, and writing the number of wangles on one of the clocks on the activity sheet.

8. Discuss with students the kind of times to be used: hours only, half hours and hours, etc. and have them complete the page.

(The following is offered for those students ready for a greater challenge.)

> Start with a time such as three o'clock and have students record the data on the activity sheet. Then ask them to find another clock angle that matches the measure of the three o'clock angle and uses the positions found on a real clock. (They should discover that nine o'clock is a match.) Have them record this next to the three o'clock. Instruct them to find pairs of matching angles as they complete the page. (Notice that the clocks on the activity sheet are arranged in pairs.) You may wish to limit students to hours and half hours.

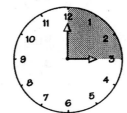 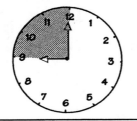

9. Discuss the activity.

Discussion

1. How did you solve the problem of making the clock? [The clock is divided into 12 hours and the wangle protractor into 24, so it takes two wangles to make each hour.]

2. How did constructing the clock help you think about the number of wangles in a certain time? (If two wangles make one hour, you could multiply the number of hours times two to find the number of wangles. Add one wangle for half hours.) Without using your protractor, how many wangles would be in 3:30? [7] ...in 7:00? [10] ...in ____?

3. For those who found angle pairs: What do you notice about the pairs of matching angles? [They are mirror images of each other; they are symmetrical.]

4. How does using the wangle protractor compare to using the wangles in *From Wedges to Wangles*? [It's easier. You don't have to work with so many pieces.]

5. How many wangles wide is your lift-top desk when it is open?

Extensions

1. Have students open their scissors as far as they will naturally go and measure the angle made by the blades. Do all scissors open the same amount? (Students may also want to check a variety of scissors at home.)

2. Use the wangle protractor to measure angles around the room. Have students list the results on a piece of chart paper.

3. Explore the two measures of the angle formed by the position of the clock hands. "Set your clock at 7:30. In how many ways could you measure this angle? [2] (Most every clock hand position allows two measuring choices. Added together the two measures should equal 24 wangles. See the illustration in *Management 4*.) Have students try some different times, take both measures, make a T-table, and discover the pattern.

time	small measure	large measure
7:30	3 wangles	21 wangles
3:00	6 wangles	18 wangles

What do you notice about the small measurements? [They are less than 12 wangles.]

Home Link

Have students use the wangle protractor to measure and record items at home.

(The wangle protractor was adapted from an idea by John A. Van de Walle in the book, *Elementary School Mathematics: Teaching Developmentally*. Longman. White Plains, New York. 1990.)

Waxed Wangles

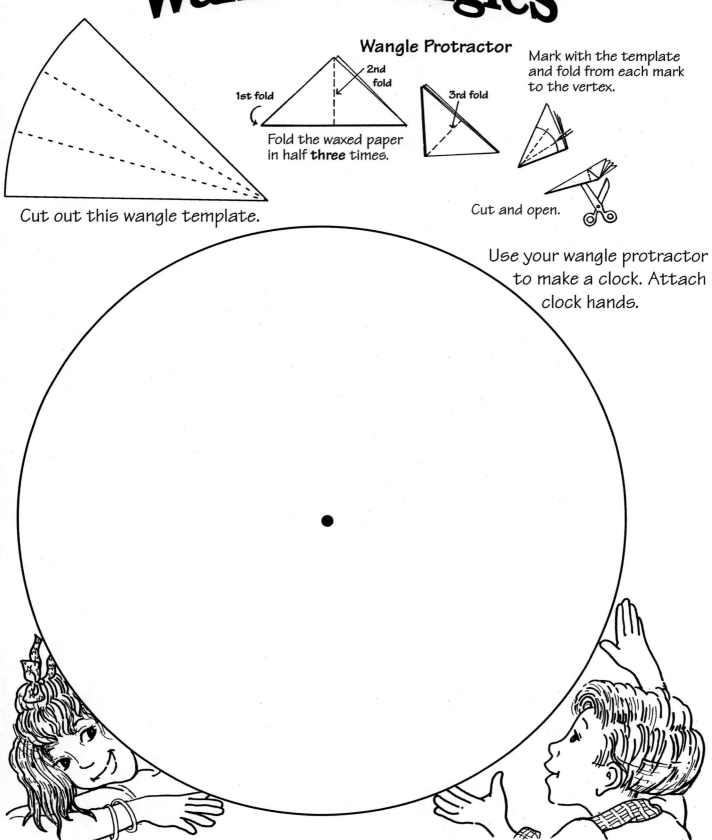

Wangle Protractor

1st fold

2nd fold

3rd fold

Fold the waxed paper in half **three** times.

Mark with the template and fold from each mark to the vertex.

Cut and open.

Cut out this wangle template.

Use your wangle protractor to make a clock. Attach clock hands.

Waxed Wangles

Show a time on the clock you made. Use your wangle protractor to measure the angle made by the clock hands. Draw the hands, shade the angle, and record the number of wangles.

Shaping Up

Topic
Geometric shapes

Key Question
How many different geometric shapes can you find as we walk around the neighborhood?

Focus
Students will observe and draw examples of geometric shapes in nature and in objects made by people.

Guiding Documents
Project 2061 Benchmarks
- *Numbers and shapes—and operations on them—help to describe and predict things about the world around us.*
- *Shapes such as circles, squares, and triangles can be used to describe many things that can be seen. (K-2)*
- *Many objects can be described in terms of simple plane figures and solids. Shapes can be compared in terms of concepts such as parallel and perpendicular, congruence and similarity, and symmetry. Symmetry can be found by reflection, turns, or slides. (3-5)*

NRC Standard
- *Objects have many observable properties, including size, weight, shape, color, temperature, and the ability to react with other substances. Those properties can be measured using tools, such as rulers, balances, and thermometers.*

NCTM Standards
- *Describe, model, draw, and classify shapes*
- *Recognize and appreciate geometry in their world*

Math
Geometry and spatial sense

Integrated Processes
Observing
Classifying
Collecting and recording data
Comparing and contrasting

Materials
Board or book to support paper while drawing
Crayons or colored pencils

Background Information
Geometric shapes are everywhere, from the foods we eat to the buildings in which we live and work. Shapes surround us at school, in the neighborhood, on the horizon, and in space.

We can gain an awareness and appreciation of the geometry in our world through observation. The more focused our observations become, the more details we notice. We then become able to connect geometric shapes and terms to all sorts of real-world settings.

To aid students in their exploration, the shapes listed in this activity have been organized into groups. This can be done in at least two ways—by dimension (1-D, 2-D, 3-D) or by characteristics (open shapes, closed shapes defining a region, closed shapes with volume). Dimension was chosen as being appropriate for students at this level.

Management
1. A walk in the surrounding neighborhood is suggested but it could also be done around the school grounds.
2. Identify the shapes for which you want students to search and have them circle those words on the first activity page. You may want them to concentrate on just one group of shapes or on only one or two shapes from each group. The page can be used at various times to look for different shapes.
3. The second activity sheet can be done on another day.

Procedure
1. Explain that the class will be taking a geometry walk. They will be looking for lines and shapes found in nature and in objects made by people.
2. Give students the first activity page and a firm writing surface such as a clipboard or book. Have them underline or circle the shapes on which you want them to focus.

3. Guide the walk, stopping frequently to give students time to draw and label their examples.
4. Return to the classroom and have students share what they found.
5. Distribute the second activity page. Instruct students to write some 1-dimensional, 2-dimensional, and 3-dimensional words in the first column. (You may want everyone in the class to use the same words.) All of the spaces need not be used.
6. Take students outside and challenge them to find an object that illustrates more than one line or shape—the more matches, the better. Have them write the name of the object above the second column and mark all the appropriate boxes. For example:

1-Dimensional

	tree
horizontal	
vertical	x
parallel	x
perpendicular	x

2-Dimensional

circle	
triangle	
square	
rectangle	

3-Dimensional

sphere	
cube	
cylinder	x

7. Have students continue by finding three more objects.
8. Ask students to explain why they marked the boxes they did. For example, "I marked *perpendicular* because the tree trunk is perpendicular to the ground." Accept all reasonable answers.

Discussion
1. What shapes were hardest to find? …easiest to find?
2. How many objects can we name that have squares? …cubes? …horizontal lines?, etc. (Make lists on chart paper or a transparency.)
3. Why did you mark the boxes you did for _____ (name object)?
4. In how many different ways can we describe a toy wagon using geometric words?
5. What object did you find most pleasing to observe? What shapes did it have?

Curriculum Correlation
Language Arts
1. Hoban, Tana. *Spirals, Curves, Fanshapes and Lines.* Greenwillow Books. New York. 1992. (This book has colorful photographs of the geometry in our world.)
2. Have students write poetry in geometric shapes.
   a. Write a poem with three lines (one word, two words, three words) in the shape of a triangle or a square poem with four lines and four words on each line.

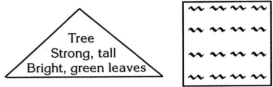

Tree
Strong, tall
Bright, green leaves

   b. Write a poem about squares inside a square, a poem about triangles inside a triangle, etc.

Art
1. Make a picture using only geometric shapes.
2. Create a collage using one shape of various sizes and colors or use a combination of one line and one shape.
3. Build three-dimensional shapes out of construction paper.

Home Link
Have students do a shape hunt around their house.

Shaping Up

Name _____

Draw and label examples of geometry in nature and in objects made by people.

1-D
(lines)
horizontal
vertical
diagonal
curve
parallel
perpendicular
intersecting

2-D
triangle
square
rectangle
pentagon
hexagon
octagon
circle

3-D
cube
cone
pyramid
cylinder
sphere
rectangular
prism

Shaping Up

Find four examples of geometry
in nature and in objects
made by people that
can be described
in several ways.

1-Dimensional

2-Dimensional

3-Dimensional

Slice Me Twice

Topic
Quadrilaterals

Key Question
What happens when we cut circles that are attached to each other?

Focus
Students will investigate how two-circle constructions are changed into various quadrilaterals and then continue with explorations of their own.

Guiding Documents
Project 2061 Benchmarks
- *Mathematics is the study of many kinds of patterns, including numbers and shapes and operations on them. Sometimes patterns are studied because they help to explain how the world works or how to solve practical problems, sometimes because they are interesting in themselves.*
- *Many objects can be described in terms of simple plane figures and solids. Shapes can be compared in terms of concepts such as parallel and perpendicular, congruence and similarity, and symmetry. Symmetry can be found by reflection, turns, or slides.*

NRC Standards
- *Plan and conduct a simple investigation.*
- *Employ simple equipment and tools to gather data and extend the senses.*
- *Communicate investigations and explanations.*

NCTM Standards
- *Investigate and predict the results of combining, subdividing, and changing shapes*
- *Develop spatial sense*
- *Describe, model, draw, and classify shapes*

Math
Geometry and spatial sense

Integrated Processes
Predicting
Observing
Collecting and recording data
Comparing and contrasting
Generalizing
Applying

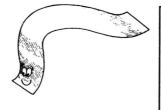

Materials
Paper strips (see *Management 1*)
Transparent tape
Scissors

Background Information
The power of this activity lies in exploration and discovery. Students are introduced to some specific two-circle constructions to investigate and then are encouraged to test ideas of their own. All of the constructions move from three-dimensions (length, width, height) to two-dimensions (length and width).

Spatial visualization is an important component of the prediction process. Students need to picture in their minds how the way the circles are constructed will determine the shape which results when the circles are cut. As more data are collected, a more accurate prediction should be possible.

Properties of Two-Circle Shapes

Rectangle	Square
quadrilateral (four sides)	rectangle/rhombus
opposite sides equal	all sides equal
opposite sides parallel	opposite sides parallel
four right angles	four right angles
Parallelogram	**Rhombus**
quadrilateral	parallelogram
opposite sides equal	all sides equal
opposite sides parallel	opposite sides parallel
opposite angles equal	opposite angles equal

Management
1. Cut paper strips at least 1 inch by 11 inches in two colors. If only one color is available, have students color strips so they have two colors. Plan on eight or more strips for each student, depending on how many explorations will be done.
2. Taping along entire edges and on both sides where strips attach to each other is extremely important.

(The following approaches are offered for those students who are ready for more independent investigations. With either approach, it is suggested students write a description/result of one of their constructions. Mount these on a bulletin board and challenge students to find ones no one has yet discovered.)

Open-ended: Challenge students to explore the *Key Question,* organize their results, and offer conclusions relating the way the circles are constructed to the shape produced when they are cut.

Guided planning: Give students the *Plan Sheet* to help them organize their investigation of the *Key Question.*

Procedure

1. Give each student two equal paper strips, one of each color. Transparent tape and scissors should be available.
2. Direct students to loop each strip into a circle and secure by taping completely across both sides.
3. Show students how to tape one circle on top of the other at 90° angles. Reach inside the top circle and tape both edges to the bottom circle. Turn it over and tape the inside edges.

4. Ask the *Key Question*. Distribute the activity sheet and have students fill in the first three columns. Have them predict the shape they will get when the circle is cut along the middle.

# of Circles	Equal or Unequal Circles	90° or 45° Angles
2	equal	90°

5. Show students how to slightly pinch one circle, snip the center, and cut all the way around the middle of the circle.
6. Instruct students to cut one of their circles. They will have a straight strip with a loop at each end. They should cut down the center of the straight piece and lay the figure flat.

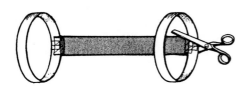

7. Students should record the shape. Discuss together the properties of the square.
8. Ask, "What will happen if we start with one circle larger than the other?"
9. Distribute more strips. Have students shorten one strip and repeat the process.
10. Ask, "What will happen if we tape the circles at a different angle?" Show them how to tape circles at a 45° angle. Then let them explore the shapes made with equal and unequal circles.
11. Discuss what has been discovered.

12. Ask, "What other circle constructions would you like to explore?" Give them more strips for their investigations.

Discussion

1. How does the way the circles are constructed affect the shape when they are cut? [taping at 90° made shapes with right angles, same length made shapes with equal sides, etc.]
2. How are the shapes (quadrilaterals) alike? ... different?
3. What other circle constructions would you like to explore?

Extensions

1. Explore the lines of symmetry and/or the characteristics of the diagonals for each quadrilateral.
2. Try other constructions such as a circle taped within a circle, three circles, four circles, etc. A particularly intriguing challenge would be to make a circle construction that will produce a triangle(s). [Two equilateral triangles (with twists) can be made by equally spacing three circles within each other. Attach only on one end of the sphere-like shape.]

Three circles   *Construction for triangles*

3. Make circle constructions using paper with differently colored sides (origami paper, wrapping paper, etc.). Compare the color placement of the construction to the results after cutting. Encourage students to find a way to make a square (or other shape) with a frame showing the same color or pattern on one side.
4. Challenge students to construct a picture frame out of paper strips that will fit one of their pieces of art work.

Curriculum Correlation
Language Arts

Write *Who Am I?* riddles using the properties of the quadrilaterals. Example: "I have four equal sides and four right angles. Who am I?"

Slice Me Twice

PLAN SHEET

What happens when we cut circles that are attached to each other?

1. How many circles do you plan to attach together?

2. Describe or draw the different circle constructions you want to try.

3. How are you going to organize your data? Will you include predictions?

4. How are you going to show your results and conclusions?

5. After doing the constructions you planned, what new ones would you like to try?

Slice Me Twice

Make circles from paper strips. Tape them together at 90° or 45° angles. Fill in the first three columns. Predict the shape that will result when the circles are cut along the middle. Try it!

# of Circles	Equal or Unequal Circles	90° or 45° Angles	Predicted Shape	Actual Shape	Properties of Shape

Möbius Bands

Topic
Möbius strips

Key Question
How do combinations of twists and cuts affect the Möbius bands?

Focus
Students will explore the Möbius band by observing the results of varying the number of twists and kind of cuts.

Guiding Documents
Project 2061 Benchmark
- *Mathematics is the study of many kinds of patterns, including numbers and shapes and operations on them. Sometimes patterns are studied because they help to explain how the world works or how to solve practical problems, sometimes because they are interesting in themselves.*

NRC Standards
- *Plan and conduct a simple investigation.*
- *Employ simple equipment and tools to gather data and extend the senses.*

NCTM Standards
- *Investigate and predict the results of combining, subdividing, and changing shapes*
- *Develop spatial sense*

Math
Geometry and spatial sense
   topology
Counting
Fractions

Integrated Processes
Predicting
Observing
Collecting and recording data
Comparing and contrasting

Materials
Paper strips (see *Management 1*)
Transparent tape
Scissors
Crayons or colored pencils

Background Information
A Möbius strip or band is a one-sided surface formed by giving a rectangular strip a half twist before joining the two ends together. It was discovered in 1858 by August Ferdinand Möbius (1790-1868), a German mathematician and astronomer. To illustrate its one-sidedness, a line can be drawn from any point on the band to any other point without crossing an edge.

An odd number of half twists will make a one-sided figure. An even number of half twists gives a two-sided figure which is not, by definition, a Möbius band. However, it is interesting to explore the results of cutting both odd and even numbers of half twists and generalize about the number of half twists needed to make a Möbius band.

While, at first glance, the Möbius band seems to be just another interesting mathematical oddity, it has applications in technology. During the time that Möbius discovered the band, the Industrial Revolution was in full swing in Europe and the United States. Many of the factories had a single power source, usually a steam engine or water wheel, which turned a long shaft, or series of shafts. The individual pieces of equipment in the factory were connected to the shafts by a series of belts and wheels. In this way a single steam engine in a cloth-weaving factory, for example, could be used to power dozens of looms. The belts connecting the individual machines to the overhead shaft were constantly turning and would have to be replaced periodically.

Plant engineers found that putting a half twist in the belts – making them into Möbius bands – made them last longer, since the belts would have to go around twice to get back to the same point of wear. Thus, Möbius' discovery was quickly applied to the technology of the day.

Möbius bands are still used in factories today, but another, more modern application has appeared with the advent of the computer. Some types of printer ribbons are Möbius bands. This can be seen if you open the ribbon cartridge from an Apple® ImageWriter®. Since it cycles through the printer twice before it gets back to the same point of wear, the half twist makes the ribbon last twice as long as a non-Möbius ribbon.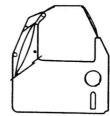

Management
1. Möbius bands can be made with any reasonable size or type of paper. Adding machine tape 18-24

inches long is easy for students to handle. Cut at least five strips for each student.

2. When forming the bands, always tape completely across both sides.

3. To make comparisons more easily, have students label the bands (after cutting) with the number of half twists and kind of cut.

(The alternate approaches which follow are offered for those students who are ready for more independent work.)

Open-ended: Introduce a Möbius band and encourage students to ask "What if...?" questions that can be explored. Have student groups plan how they will record and report their findings.

Guided planning: Introduce a Möbius band and encourage students to ask "What if...?" questions that can be explored. As students meet in planning groups, guide them with the following questions.
1. What are the variables you are going to test?
2. What kind of cuts do you want to try?
3. How are you going to test for one-sidedness?
4. Set up a way to record your data, including predictions.
5. What are the responsibilities of each member of your group?
6. After carrying out your plan, what patterns did you discover?
7. Which band and cut, in your opinion, gave the most fascinating result?

Procedure
1. Distribute the activity sheet, paper strips, transparent tape, scissors, and crayons.
2. Have students label each end of the strips with letters.

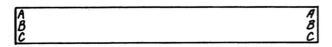

3. Direct students to use the first strip to make a band with no twists. The letters should meet on the same side. Tape the ends together completely across both sides of the strip.
4. Instruct students to take one crayon and draw down the center of the band until they connect to their starting point. Then have students take another color and do the same on the other side. Ask, "How many sides does this band have?" [Two.] Have them put this data in the table.
5. Have students predict what will happen when they cut along the line.
6. Show students how to slightly pinch the band, snip the center, and cut down the middle. Have them cut their own bands and record the results by describing or drawing.

7. Have students make a second band. Before taping, give one end a half twist. A blank end will meet a lettered end.
8. Challenge students to show the number of sides by again drawing lines with their crayons. Ask, "What did you discover?" Explain that this is a Möbius band; it has only one side.
9. Instruct students to make a prediction about the results of cutting down the center of the band. They should complete the cut and record their results.

10. Students should make another band, again with one half twist. Have them predict what will happen when they cut it *one-third* of the way from the edge instead of along the center.

11. Have students make the cut and record the results. (They will need to cut around the band two complete times.)
12. Invite students to try different numbers of half twists and cuts on their own.
13. Hold a concluding discussion, including how the Möbius band is being applied in the real world (see *Background Information*).

Discussion
1. Look at your bands with one half twist. How do the results of the 1/2 cut compare with those of the 1/3 cut? [1/2 cut: one band twice as long as the original, 1/3 cut: two bands, one the same length as the original and the other twice as long]
2. What patterns did you discover?
3. How are the number of half twists related to the number of sides of the band? When were the bands one-sided? [odd number of half twists makes one-sided bands, even number makes two-sided bands]
4. Which band and cut, in your opinion, gave the most fascinating result?
5. What else would you like to try?

Extensions

1. Cut a half twist band 1/4 of the way from the edge.
2. Do *Slice Me Twice* constructions with Möbius bands.
3. Teacher demonstration: Cut two identical paper strips. Place them on top of each other, make a half twist and tape the top end to the top end and the bottom end to the bottom end. Slide a pen between the bands to show that they are two separate pieces. Then open it up. Surprised?

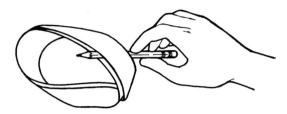

Curriculum Correlation
Language Arts

Share this limerick:

A mathematician confided
That a Möbius band is one-sided,
And you'll get quite a laugh
If you cut one in half,
For it stays in one piece when divided.
— Author Unknown

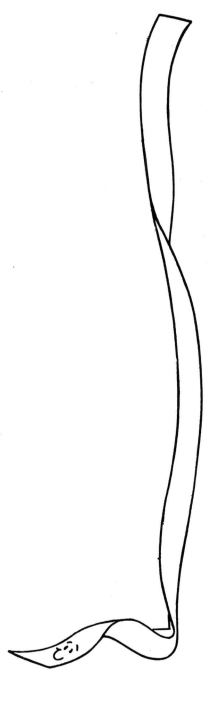

Möbius Bands

How do combinations of twists and cuts affect the Möbius bands?

$\frac{1}{2}$ cut ----------------

$\frac{1}{3}$ cut ----------------

Start with these explorations.
Then try more of your own.

# of $\frac{1}{2}$ Twists	# of Sides	Kind of Cut	Prediction	Results (length, width, # loops)
0		$\frac{1}{2}$		
1		$\frac{1}{2}$		
1		$\frac{1}{3}$		

GEO-PANES

Topic
Geometric figures
Minimum surfaces

Key Question
What kind of geo-pane (soap film pattern) will form on a three-dimensional shape?

Focus
Students will discover and appreciate the unique soap film patterns that form inside polyhedrons.

Guiding Documents
Project 2061 Benchmarks
- *Mathematics is the study of many kinds of patterns, including numbers and shapes and operations on them. Sometimes patterns are studied because they help to explain how the world works or how to solve practical problems, sometimes because they are interesting in themselves.*
- *Use numerical data in describing and comparing objects and events.*

NRC Standards
- *Employ simple equipment and tools to gather data and extend the senses.*
- *Communicate investigations and explanations.*

NCTM Standards
- *Describe, model, draw, and classify shapes*
- *Recognize and appreciate geometry in their world*

Math
Geometry and spatial sense
Counting

Science
Physical science
      matter

Integrated Processes
Predicting
Observing
Collecting and recording data
Comparing and contrasting
Generalizing

Materials
For the class:
    liquid dish soap
    1 spool of thread or paper clips
    vinegar
    1 or more old towels, *optional*
    liter and 15 ml measures, *optional*
    newspaper and scratch paper, *optional*

For each group:
    clay (see *Management 2*)
    toothpicks
    1 container such as a half-gallon milk carton

Background Information
Geo-panes are defined as the pattern of *panes*, or soap film, created by dipping shapes into a water and soap solution. Patterns which might be expected to form around the sides of the polyhedrons meet, instead, near the center. The elastic, rubbery skin (surface tension) of the soap film stretches to cover the smallest possible area or minimum surface. Less area is covered when the soap film comes toward the center than if it were to cover the faces around the geometric shape.

The activity begins with the triangle and the square. They have two dimensions, length and width. A third dimension, height, is added when the tetrahedron, cube, triangular prism, and pyramid are built. These three-dimensional shapes are also known as polyhedrons, many-sided figures.

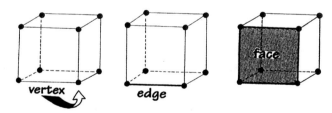

Students might also explore the relationship between vertices, edges, and faces for the polyhedrons they made. The formula, called Euler's (pronounced *oilers*) Theorem, states that **vertices + faces = edges + 2.** This is true for all convex polyhedrons. These are polyhedrons whose frameworks, if covered, have no indentations.

Shapes	2-D		3-D			
	△	☐				
# of Vertices (points)	3	4	4	8	6	5
# of Edges (line segments)	3	4	6	12	9	8
# of Faces (sides)	1	1	4	6	5	5

Management

1. This activity will take about 60 to 90 minutes.
2. All figures are made using whole toothpicks.
3. To anchor the toothpicks at the vertices, use oil-based (plasticine) clay rolled into 1 cm balls. Scratch paper helps protect desks while rolling clay. You may prefer to use raisins or dry legumes (soak several hours to soften) instead of clay.
4. Groups of three or four should build the four polyhedrons shown on the activity sheet, each member being responsible for at least one.
5. Spread newspaper over the dipping area (tables or floor), preferably away from desks. Dipping can be done outside if the air is still.
6. For each container, pour water to a depth of no less than 9 cm, add a good squirt of liquid soap, and stir gently so bubbles do not form. If you prefer, have students measure about one liter of water and 15 ml of soap for each container. Another 15 ml of granulated sugar or glycerin (found in drugstores) may be added to strengthen the solution.
7. Caution students to dip carefully so the surface of the soapy water stays relatively free of foam and bubbles. Skim them off if necessary. The bubbles can make it difficult to see the pattern or can actually change it.
8. Students will want to experiment with more complex designs of their own. Suggest they use smaller sections of toothpicks for these.
9. To cut through the soapy film when cleaning up, sprinkle some vinegar on the wet areas and rub dry.

Procedure

1. Give each student a small lump of clay, about 12 toothpicks, about 50 cm of thread, and the activity sheet.
2. Have each student build a square or triangle with the toothpicks and clay. They should record the number of vertices and edges.
3. Borrow a triangle and dip it in the soapy water. Explain that, for this activity, the resulting pane will be called a *geo-pane*. Students should record that it has one face or flat surface. Repeat with the square. Students might notice that both two-dimensional shapes have one face.
4. Ask students to predict what will happen when they dip a three-dimensional shape in the soapy water. Give students a chance to verbalize their ideas before writing their predictions.
5. Instruct students to use their triangle or square to build one of the three-dimensional shapes. Each group should decide who will build which shape so that all of the polyhedrons shown are represented.
6. Have students record the number of vertices, edges, and faces for these shapes *before* they go

anywhere near the soapy water. Help them determine the number of faces, if needed, as this may be a new term to them.
7. Show students how to slip the thread under one, and only one, toothpick and hold the thread by both ends as shown on the activity sheet. Do not tie the thread to the toothpick.
8. Students should carry their shapes to the dipping area and take turns completely submerging them in the soapy water. They should dip each shape several times to see if the pattern stays the same. Students will likely want to build and try additional shapes.
9. Hold a concluding discussion and have students write about what happened.

Discussion

1. Which of the three-dimensional shapes started with a triangular base? [tetrahedron, maybe the triangular prism (Don't insist students use these terms.)] Which started with a square base? [cube, pyramid]
2. What other shapes did you build and test?
3. Is the geo-pane pattern the same each time? [usually, but a change in conditions – soap bubbles, wind, etc. – can cause differences]
4. How could you change the geo-pane pattern? [change the thread position, pop one pane, blow on it, etc.]
5. How did you feel when you saw the geo-panes? Which was your favorite geo-pane pattern? (Students may not be able to pick just one.)
6. What other shapes would you like to try?

Extension

Challenge students to study the three-dimensional section of the table to find a relationship between vertices, edges, and faces (see *Background Information*).

Curriculum Correlation

Art

Have students construct polyhedrons such as cubes, tetrahedrons, and pyramids using paper patterns and glue. This is also a good preliminary activity.

Technology

Students might create three-dimensional geometric figures on the computer using *Logo*.

GEO-PANES

What kind of geo-pane will form
on a 3-D shape?

Build these shapes and complete the table.

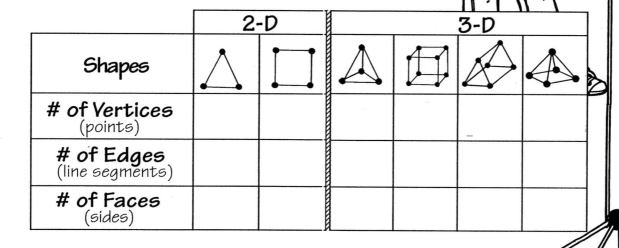

Shapes	2-D		3-D			
# of Vertices (points)						
# of Edges (line segments)						
# of Faces (sides)						

Hang each shape from a thread and dip
completely into soapy water. Lift it out
and observe.

• What do you think will happen?

• What did happen?

80   © 1996 AIMS Education Foundation

Edge to Edge

Topic
Polyominoes

Key Questions
1. In how many ways can squares be joined together?
2. How many different patterns can be made with five squares?

Focus
Students will explore various polyominoes and eventually discover the twelve pentomino shapes.

Guiding Documents
Project 2061 Benchmarks
- *Mathematics is the study of many kinds of patterns, including numbers and shapes and operations on them. Sometimes patterns are studied because they help to explain how the world works or how to solve practical problems, sometimes because they are interesting in themselves.*
- *Some features of things may stay the same even when other features change. Some patterns look the same when they are shifted over, or turned, or reflected, or seen from different directions.*

NRC Standards
- *Plan and conduct a simple investigation.*
- *Communicate investigations and explanations.*

NCTM Standards
- *Investigate and predict the results of combining, subdividing, and changing shapes*
- *Recognize and appreciate geometry in their world*

Math
Geometry and spatial sense
Patterns

Integrated Processes
Observing
Predicting
Collecting and recording data
Comparing and contrasting

Materials
Scissors
Crayons or colored pencils
Square tiles, optional (see *Management 1*)
Envelopes, optional (see *Management 2*)

Background Information
In how many ways can squares be joined together? Following certain rules (see below), this question can launch students on a journey of discovery. By exploring the patterns of one to four squares, students will have a basis for making predictions and finding all of the five-square patterns or pentominoes. No formula has yet been derived for mathematically determining how many polyominoes are possible for a given number of connected squares.

# of patterns	# of patterns	Patterns
1 (monomino)	1	□
2 (domino)	1	▢▢
3 (tromino)	2	▢▢▢ ⌐
4 (tetromino)	5	
5 (pentomino)	12	
6 (hexomino)	35	

Rules for joining squares
1. Squares must touch along one entire edge.

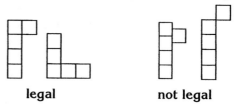

legal   **not legal**

2. If a pattern can fit on top of another using a flip or turn, it is considered to be the same. For example, the patterns below are the same.

Management

1. Make copies of the square grid on colored construction paper, one per student plus a few extra. Students should cut five individual squares from the construction paper or be provided with five square tiles.
2. Envelopes may be used to store pentomino pieces for later puzzle work or for doing the related activity, *Net-Sense*.
3. The overhead projector is a helpful tool for demonstrating the rules for joining squares as well as showing results. Have available five squares to manipulate on the projector.

(The following is offered for those students ready for more independent work.)

> *Open-ended:* Ask students, "In how many ways can one to five squares be joined together?" Give them the rules and five squares. Have them devise their own means of representing and reporting the data.

Procedure

1. Give students five square tiles or distribute the square grid and have students cut out five squares.
2. Ask the first *Key Question*, "In how many ways can squares be joined?" Demonstrate the rules for joining squares.
3. Once students have the first activity sheet, have them find and record all the ways to join one square.
4. Instruct students to move two of their squares into all of the possible positions and record. Repeat for three squares and four squares.
5. Ask students the second *Key Question*, "How many different patterns can be made with five squares?" Direct students to record their predictions.
6. Have students explore the five-square patterns and record by coloring in the 5x3 grids on the activity sheet. The emphasis is on discovery; do not give any clues as to how many pentominoes can be made. Toward the end of the discovery period, you may ask questions such as "Who can find the 13th pentomino?" so exploration will continue until the students are absolutely convinced all the pentominoes have been found. Encourage perseverance.
7. Direct students to use the square grid paper to cut out the pentomino pieces they have identified. Encourage them to conserve space. However some will need a second sheet to finish.
8. Discuss their findings. Have students hold up like pieces to make sure their set is complete. It is helpful to give each shape a letter name such as

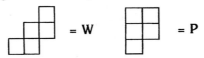

9. Invite students to store pentominoes in envelopes for further investigations or extensions.

Discussion

1. How did you go about searching for all the pentomino pieces? (just moved the squares a lot of different ways until I came up with something new, trial and error)
2. How could you conduct the pentomino search in an orderly way? [explore all the possibilities with five squares in a row, then four squares in a row, three squares in a row, etc.]
3. What do you wonder about after doing this activity?

Extensions

1. The area of every pentomino is the same—five square units. How do the perimeters compare? To measure perimeters, have the edge of a square equal one unit. (The pentomino below has a perimeter of 12.)

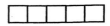

2. Challenge students to use all twelve pentomino pieces to make a rectangle. This is *not* a simple task. A 6x10 unit rectangle is included; it has over 1,000 solutions. There are also solutions for 5x12, 4x15, and 3x20 rectangles. The rectangles are measured in units, one unit being the edge of a square.

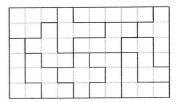

One 6x10 solution

3. Explore the three-dimensional possibilities of pentominoes by doing the activity, *Net-Sense*.
4. Have students find all of the hexominoes (six squares). Collect and display them.

Curriculum Correlation

Art

1. Suggest students trace the same pentomino piece four times to make a pattern pleasing to the eye. Does it have one or more lines of symmetry? Check with mirrors. Does it rotate around a center point?
2. Have students choose one pentomino piece and decide what it could become, perhaps by adding legs, leaves, wheels, etc. Trace around it and incorporate the shape into a picture. Write a story to go with the drawing.

Technology

Have students write *Logo* programs for the pentomino shapes.

Edge to Edge

Edge to Edge

In how many ways can these squares be joined?

# of squares	# of patterns	Drawings of patterns
1		
2		
3		
4		

How many different patterns can be made with five squares?

Prediction: Actual:

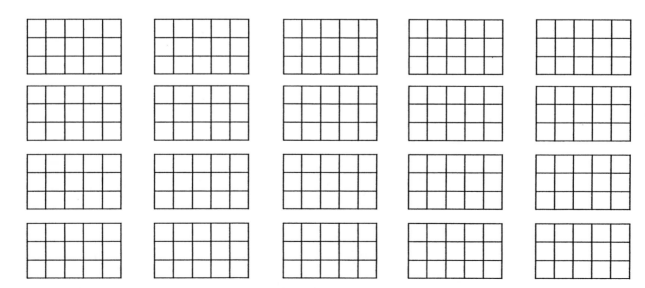

     84

Edge to Edge

Net-Sense

Topic
Pentominoes/
spatial visualization

Key Questions
1. Which pentomino nets can be folded into open boxes?
2. Which nets can be cut from an open milk carton?

Focus
Students will move from two-dimensional to three-dimensional objects and back again as they explore pentominoes which form open boxes.

Guiding Documents
NRC Standards
- *Plan and conduct a simple investigation.*
- *Communicate investigations and explanations.*

NCTM Standards
- *Investigate and predict the results of combining, subdividing, and changing shapes*
- *Develop spatial sense*

Math
Geometry and spatial sense

Integrated Processes
Observing
Predicting
Collecting and recording data
Comparing and contrasting

Materials
Part 1
    one set of pentominoes for each student
    scissors
    crayons

Part 2
    2 half-pint milk cartons for each student
    scissors
    crayons
    chart-sized paper for each group
    glue

Background Information
We want to give children many opportunities to build spatial knowledge — to explore the characteristics of two- and three-dimensional shapes, to see shapes in relationship to each other, and to examine the effects that changes have on shapes. The visual and tactile senses are employed as we construct, draw, compare, and transform things. Spatial visualization, the mental construction and manipulation of objects, is a component of spatial knowledge. This ability is being exercised and strengthened as students predict which pentominoes can be folded into open boxes and as they plan how to cut their milk carton down into pentomino nets.

A net is a pattern for building a shape or object. A one-dimensional net can be used to construct a two-dimensional shape. For example, connected lines form a square. A two-dimensional net creates a three-dimensional object. Certain pentominoes are two-dimensional nets for three-dimensional open boxes. A net creates an object one dimension higher than the net itself.

1-D net→2-D square   2-D net → 3-D open box

Students will discover that eight pentominoes can be folded into open boxes. Conversely, the milk cartons can be cut down into the same eight pentomino nets. We want students to connect the folding up results of *Part 1* with the cutting down results of *Part 2* and realize that they are just approaching the problem from two different points of view. If this link is made, they will know if they have found all the ways to cut down a milk carton or which ones they still need to find.

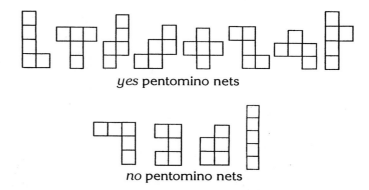

yes pentomino nets

no pentomino nets

Management

1. Have students use the pentomino set assembled while doing the activity *Edge to Edge*, or cut pentomino sets from the sheet provided.
2. You may wish to do *Part 1* and *Part 2* on different days. Groups of four are desirable for *Part 2*.
3. Have students save their lunch milk cartons for a couple of days. The cartons should be rinsed and left to dry. Collect extra milk cartons, just in case they are needed.

Procedure

Part 1

1. Have students gather their sets of pentominoes. Make sure everyone has all twelve pieces by holding up one pentomino at a time and having each student hold up the matching one.
2. Ask the first *Key Question* and distribute *Part 1*. Explain that a net, in this case, is the pattern for making a three-dimensional figure.
3. Instruct students to *mentally* fold each pentomino pictured in the giraffe's neck into a box. If they predict *yes*, have them color that pentomino piece on the paper.
4. Direct students to fold their paper pentominoes along the lines and draw the successful nets in the *YES* area and the unsuccessful nets in the *NO* area.
5. Discuss the results and have students save their paper pentominoes for *Part 2*.

Part 2

6. Ask the second *Key Question* and distribute *Part 2* along with the milk cartons.
7. Have students cut the cartons so the sides are nearly square. Challenge them to trace a path that follows the edges or folds and will make the carton lie flat.
8. Instruct students to cut along their tracing until they have a flat pattern. They may have to add or subtract cuts from the path they traced.
9. Have students take their second milk carton and try to cut a different net.
10. Direct the groups to assemble their nets and compare. How many different nets did they make? Do they think there are others?
11. Give each group a large piece of paper and have they make a display of the *yes* paper pentominoes, the *no* paper pentominoes, and their milk carton nets.
12. Encourage each group to study their display, then answer the two questions on the activity sheet.

Discussion

1. Compare the number of pentominoes that form open boxes with the total number of pentominoes.

(Have students express their answer as a fraction, 8/12, and/or make a hand-drawn circle graph.)
2. Do the pentominoes in the *no* group have something in common which makes it impossible to form an open box?
3. How many cuts did you need to make to flatten the milk carton? [4] Did it always take the same number of cuts? [Yes.]
4. How many different milk carton nets were found? (There should be eight.) Did we find them all? How do you know? (see *Discussion 5*)
5. How are the milk carton nets related to the folded paper pentominoes? (They should match because they are just the reverse process of each other. One you fold up, the other you cut down. This is one way to find if any nets are missing among the cartons.)

Extensions

1. Explore lines of symmetry. Which pentominoes can be folded in half so that one side fits on the other? Mark the folds that work.
2. Design a net that will fold into a cube. Test it.

Net-Sense

Cut these pentomino nets.

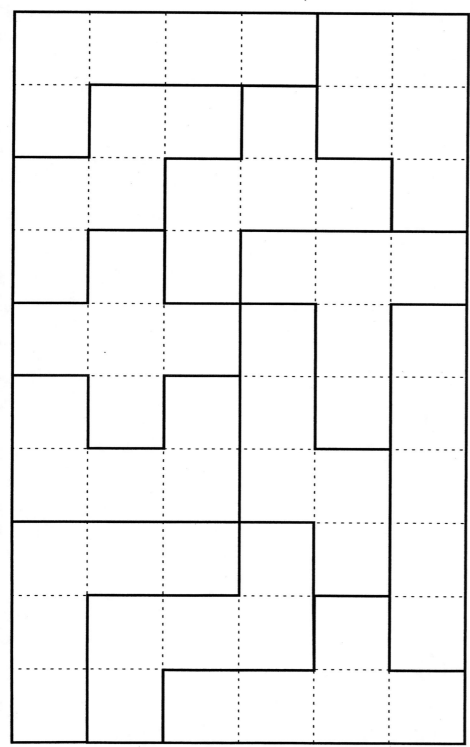

Net-Sense

Part 1

Predict by coloring.

Which pentomino nets can be folded into open boxes?

YES

NO

Name _____

Net-Sense
Part 2

Which nets can be cut from an open milk carton?

With a crayon, trace the edges you want to cut on your milk carton. Cut and draw the net you made.

Use another milk carton to make a different net. Draw it.

Working as a team. . .

How many different nets did your group make?

Make a display of your three collections:
- pentominoes that form boxes
- pentominoes that do not form boxes
- milk carton nets

What do you observe?

What new questions do you have?

Wreck-Tangles

Topic
Perimeter/area of rectangles

Key Question
How do the areas of rectangles with equal perimeters compare?

Focus
Students will discover that rectangles with equal perimeters do not necessarily have equal areas. They may also find that length times width equals area for the rectangles they tested.

Guiding Documents
Project 2061 Benchmarks
- *Length can be thought of as unit lengths joined together, area as a collection of unit squares, and volume as a set of unit cubes.*
- *Use numerical data in describing and comparing objects and events.*

NRC Standards
- *Plan and conduct a simple investigation.*
- *Employ simple equipment and tools to gather data and extend the senses.*
- *Communicate investigations and explanations.*

NCTM Standards
- *Relate geometric ideas to number and measurement ideas*
- *Understand the attributes of length, capacity, weight, mass, area, volume, time, temperature, and angle*
- *Collect, organize, and describe data*

Math
Measurement
    length
    area
Geometry and spatial sense
Order

Integrated Processes
Observing
Collecting and recording data
Comparing and contrasting
Generalizing

Materials
For each group:
    about a 32 cm length of string
    4 push pins
    1 cardboard box (see *Management 2*)
    transparent tape

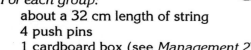

Background Information
This activity is designed to enrich students' concepts of perimeter and area. To give students a tactile experience with perimeter, they start by maneuvering string into different rectangular positions on a centimeter grid. As students move to drawing rectangles on paper, various approaches may be observed. Some will draw rectangles with a given perimeter by trial and error, erasing lines as they go. Others will realize that one length plus one width equals half of the perimeter they want. Building upon their experience with the string perimeter, some might draw rectangles in an organized way. For instance, for a perimeter of 12, they might start with a 1x5 rectangle, then a 2x4 rectangle, etc. Let students make the connections naturally; some will not be ready to move out of the trial-and-error mode.

Having examined the data, students may think they have the definitive answer such as *rectangles with equal perimeters do not have equal areas* or *length times width equals area*. But their generalizations require further testing. Will the same results be true for perimeters of 24? Can examples be found that do not confirm their generalizations?

One of the big ideas of mathematics is maximum and minimum. The length and width that are the same or closest to being the same give the maximum area for a given perimeter. In contrast, the minimum area is formed where the length and width differ by the greatest amount. Using whole numbers and a perimeter of 12, the largest area is formed by a 3x3 rectangle and the smallest area is formed by a 1x5 rectangle.

Management
1. The teacher may wish to pre-tie the string into 30-centimeter loops. Colored string or crochet thread is a nice contrast to the white paper.
2. Beforehand, have each group of three bring a cardboard box whose bottom is a little larger than an 8 1/2"x11" piece of paper.
3. *Part 1* uses centimeters as the unit of measure. The perimeters in *Part 2*, are measured in units, one unit being the edge of a square. Each square, then, represents one square unit of area.
4. *Part 2* is designed for repeated use. A good initial perimeter length to explore is 12. Then try other even numbers such as 18, 24, or whatever you wish.
5. To find the area, students should count the squares inside each rectangle. (The area formula may be one of the insights gained from this activity; it should not be imposed on students as they are in the process of discovery.)

Procedure

Part 1

1. Distribute the pre-tied 30-cm string loops to each group, along with *Part 1* and four push pins.
2. Explain that the string could represent a fence around a property, a perimeter. Have students take turns using two fingers of each hand to make different kinds of rectangles with the string.
3. Ask, "Did the length of your perimeter change when you made the different rectangles?" [No.] "I wonder if the amount of space (area) inside the rectangles changed. Let's find out!"

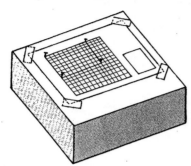

4. Have them turn their cardboard box upside-down and tape the paper to the bottom of it. Direct them to insert a push pin where it says, "Start here." This pin should not be moved during the activity.
5. Instruct students to put the string loop around the base of the push pin and put the other push pins at centimeter intersections so that the thinnest rectangle possible is formed. Have them record length, width, and area.
6. Have students continue to make other rectangles by moving the three push pins to different positions.
7. Discuss the results. Is there an organized way to find all the possible rectangles? Did anyone do it that way? What patterns do you see in the table?

Part 2

8. Distribute *Part 2* and decide what perimeter length to explore.
9. Have students draw as many different rectangles with the given perimeter as possible. Students should label the length, width, and area for each rectangle.

10. Challenge students to find a way to order their rectangles and record them in the table in this order. (They might order by increasing length, increasing width, or increasing area.) If they need more room, have them use the back of the paper.
11. Hold a concluding discussion.

Discussion

1. How did you go about finding different rectangles with perimeters of ___? (Have students reflect on the process they used: trial and error, finding one length plus one width that equal half of the perimeter, drawing rectangles in an orderly way, etc.)
2. How many different rectangles did you make?
3. Do any of your rectangles match? (Matches will occur if a 1x5 and a 5x1 are considered to be different rectangles.) Explain how they match. [Their areas are the same. If you cut one rectangle out, it would fit on top of the other rectangle.]
4. Do you consider a 2x4 rectangle the same or different from a 4x2 rectangle? Explain. (Accept any reasonable answers. As a class, decide which definition will be used when examining the results and drawing conclusions.)
5. How did you order your rectangles in the table? In what other ways could they be ordered? [by increasing length, increasing width, or increasing area]
6. What other patterns do you see in your table? [length x width = area; the closer the rectangle is to a square, the larger its area, etc.]
7. If you had the materials for ___ (name the perimeter number used) meters of fencing, what rectangle would give you the largest enclosed area? [The one closest to a square shape or with length and width nearly the same.] What rectangle would give you the smallest enclosed area? [The one where the length and width differ by the greatest amount.] Which would you rather have for a play area? [The one nearest to a square because there would be more room to play.]
8. What conclusions can you make based on your data? (Examples: Rectangles with equal perimeters do not have equal areas. Length times width equals area. When the length and width are the same or nearly the same, the area will be the largest for a given perimeter. The length and width that differ by the greatest amount will have the smallest area for a given perimeter.) In what ways could you test your conclusions?

Extensions

1. Repeat this activity with a different perimeter. This allows continued testing of generalizations and reinforces their feel for the area formula.
2. Investigate whether a rectangle can be made from a odd-numbered perimeter.

Wreck-Tangles
Part 1

How do the areas of rectangles
with equal perimeters compare?

Make a
string loop with
a perimeter of 30 cm. Tape this paper
to a box and use push pins to make
different rectangles.

Length	Width	Area

Start Here

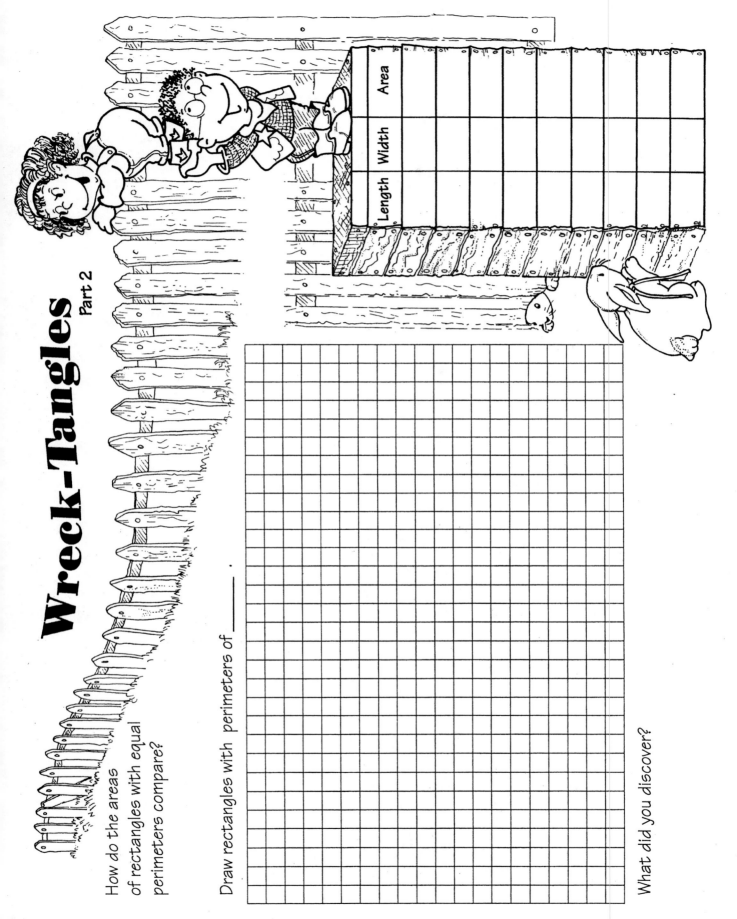

Wreck-Tangles
Part 2

How do the areas of rectangles with equal perimeters compare?

Length	Width	Area

Draw rectangles with perimeters of _____.

What did you discover?

Paper Pinchers

Topic
Exploring area through origami

Key Question
How does the area of a square change as it is folded?

Focus
Students will fold squares in various ways and determine how the areas are related to each other.

Guiding Documents
Project 2061 Benchmarks
- *Mathematics is the study of many kinds of patterns, including numbers and shapes and operations on them. Sometimes patterns are studied because they help to explain how the world works or how to solve practical problems, sometimes because they are interesting in themselves.*
- *Measurements are always likely to give slightly different numbers, even if what is being measured stays the same.*
- *Length can be thought of as unit lengths joined together, area as a collection of unit squares, and volume as a set of unit cubes.*
- *Many objects can be described in terms of simple plane figures and solids. Shapes can be compared in terms of concepts such as parallel and perpendicular, congruence and similarity, and symmetry. Symmetry can be found by reflection, turns, or slides.*

NRC Standards
- *Employ simple equipment and tools to gather data and extend the senses.*
- *Communicate investigations and explanations.*

NCTM Standards
- *Use patterns and relationships to analyze mathematical situations*
- *Relate geometric ideas to number and measurement ideas*
- *Explore transformations of geometric figures*

Math
Counting
Measurement
 length
Using formulas
 area
Geometry and spatial sense
Patterns

Integrated Processes
Observing
Predicting
Collecting and recording data
Comparing and contrasting
Generalizing

Materials
For each student:
 several squares of thin paper (see *Management 1*)
 metric ruler

For the teacher:
 optional: wax paper squares

Background Information
 Geometry is rich with patterns pulled from the real world yet, too often, it occupies a subservient position to other strands of mathematics. Some of its power and activity-based potential can be realized through the use of origami, a craft to which students are naturally attracted.

 A square piece of paper is the traditional base for origami projects. In this activity we investigate the effect folds have on the area of a figure – first with half folds, then with folds that make increasingly smaller squares. The tactile experiences with geometric patterns, linked to the number patterns generated by measurement, provide students with a helpful foundation for building concepts.

 Origami literally means paper folding (*ori*-to fold, *gami*–paper). In its purest form, no cutting or pasting is allowed. Evidence of origami dates back about 1,000 years. Although it was nurtured and popularized in Japan, origami enthusiasts today are scattered across the world, particularly in Spain, South America, and the United States. It was first used to make elaborate paper ornaments to attach to ceremonial gifts (*noshi*) but has now become more of a recreational activity. New folds and creative ways to use origami continue to be discovered.

 Japanese children are often taught origami when they are five or six years old. A child who has become proficient at paper folding is challenged to use increasingly smaller pieces of paper such as candy wrappers.

Management
1. Cut paper squares from newsprint, copy paper, graph paper, new or used wrapping paper, etc. Consider using graph paper with an even number

of squares for *Explorations with One Fold*. A 20-cm square is recommended for *Explorations with Sets of Folds*. Paper squares of any size or kind can be used for the origami figures, but origami paper is preferrable for the *Fancy Box* because of the patterning effect that is created. (See the *Oral Instructions* at the end of the teacher's text for further directions.)

2. Practice making the origami figures before presenting the activity.

3. Most students will benefit from a step-by-step visual demonstration of the origami folds. Use wax paper squares on the overhead to effectively show each step; students can see the degrees of shading as layers are folded.

4. A much more challenging option is to give the origami instructions orally (see *Oral Instructions* at the end of the teacher's text).

5. A valley fold goes inward. A mountain fold forms a peak.

valley fold   **mountain fold**

Procedure
Explorations with One Fold

1. Ask the *Key Question*.

2. Distribute the first activity sheet and a square piece of paper. Students should find all the ways to fold the square in half and draw the results on the grid.

3. Have students shade, count, and record the number of grid squares on one side of the fold line.

4. Instruct students to write a statement comparing the areas of the shaded parts along with an explanation.

5. Challenge students to find another way to prove that the shaded areas are the same and draw or describe it on the activity sheet. (Hints: cut the triangle so that it can be superimposed on the rectangle, measure the rectangle and triangle and use formulas to find their areas)

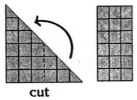

cut

6. Discuss the questions on the activity sheet (also see *Discussion 1* and *2*).

Explorations with Sets of Folds

7. Distribute the second activity sheet. Students may use the square paper from the previous exploration or a new one.

8. Direct students to measure the length and width of the open square to the nearest millimeter. They should find the area by an appropriate method and record in the table.

9. Have students make the first set of folds, complete the measurement, and record results in the table. Repeat for the second and third sets of folds.

10. Instruct students to study the table and record any patterns that are found.

11. Using the patterns, have students predict the length, width, and area of a fourth fold.

12. Guide a class discussion (see *Discussion 3* through *5*).

Explorations with Origami

13. Give each student a square paper for each origami figure they will make.

14. Have students fold one or more origami figures by watching a step-by-step demonstration, using the illustrations on the activity sheet or listening to the *Oral Instructions* at the end of the teacher's text.

15. Hold a concluding class discussion (see *Discussion 6* through *9*).

Discussion
Explorations with One Fold

1. By folding a square in half, we found lines of symmetry. How many lines of symmetry does a square have? [4]

2. How does the perimeter change when the square is folded in half? Does it change in the same way that the area does?

Explorations with Sets of Folds

3. How do the measurements within the class compare? What might cause differences? [degree of accuracy in measuring, accuracy in folding the square]

4. What patterns did you find in the table? [In every other set of folds, the length and width are cut in half. The area is reduced by half with each set of folds.] *The pattern may not be perfect but should be close enough to detect.*

5. What should the measurements of the fourth fold be? [length and width should be half of the second set of folds, area should be half of the third set of folds]

Explorations with Origami

6. What kinds of geometric shapes can you find in your origami figures?

7. Which figure was the easiest to make? ... most difficult?

8. What other figures can you create with this base?

9. Who folded a figure with the smallest piece of paper? What size was your paper? Which figure did you choose to make? Why?

Extensions

1. Find the total area of the servant.

2. Calculate how many square pieces of paper had to be cut for the class to do this activity.

3. Discuss the kinds of triangles (isosceles, equilateral, scalene, right) made by the folds.
4. Use a protractor to measure the angles of the various folded shapes.

Curriculum Correlation
Art
   Gather ideas for other origami or paper-folding projects and continue the exploration.

Literature
   Coerr, Eleanor. *Sadako and the Thousand Paper Cranes.* Putnam. 1977. After reading this book, learn how to fold the crane, a classic origami figure.

Home Link
   Have students teach family members to make one of the origami figures.

Oral Instructions

Servant
1. Find the center of the square by folding it in half twice, each in a different direction. Open to the original square.
2. Bring each corner to the center and crease.
3. Turn the square over and repeat step 2.
4. Again turn the square over and repeat step 2.
5. Turn over. Open three of the four small squares by gently pulling up and out from the center slits. Flatten them to form rectangles.
6. Draw a face on the remaining square.

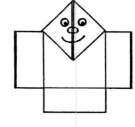

3-D Star
If using origami paper, start with the colored side facing you.
1. Find the center of the square by folding it in half twice, each in a different direction. Open to the original square.
2. Bring each corner to the center and crease.
3. Turn the square over and repeat step 2.
4. Turn the square to the side showing four squares.
5. Take each corner at the center and fold it back to the outside corner of the large square, forming a triangle.
6. Make a valley fold diagonally across the whole figure. Open and repeat along the other diagonal. Open.
7. Make a mountain fold across the center and parallel to the sides of the whole figure. Open and repeat in the other direction. Open.
8. Lift the bottom edge of each corner triangle apart from the base and pinch the triangle into a mountain fold matching the diagonal of the whole figure.

Fancy box
Origami paper is recommended. Start with the white side facing you.
1. Find the center of the square by folding it in half twice, each in a different direction. Open to the original square.
2. Bring each corner to the center and crease.
3. Turn the square over and repeat step 2.
4. Fold each triangle back so that the fold line is parallel with the edge of the square and the point of the triangle extends slightly beyond the square.
5. The folds you made in the previous step form the outline of a square. Crease this square downward.
6. Turn the whole figure to the side showing four squares.
7. Take each corner at the center and fold it back to the outside corner of the large square, forming a triangle.
8. Starting at the base of the triangle (the diagonal fold you just made), pleat the top paper back and forth until you have formed a border at the diagonal. Repeat for all corners.
9. Lift each corner triangle upward and pinch so that the pleated border is creased in half. Make a perpendicular fold extending from the crease of the border to the base of the figure. Repeat for all corners.

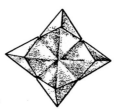

Paper Pinchers

Explorations with One Fold

Find all the possible ways to fold a square in half. For each one, draw a 6 x 6 square on the grid below. Shade the squares on one side of the fold. Count the shaded squares to find the area. Record.

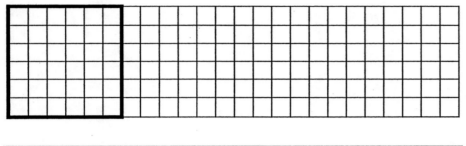

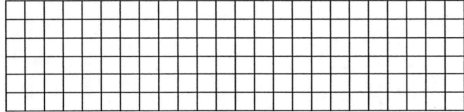

What did you notice? How would you explain that?

In what other ways, besides counting, can you show how the areas of the folded shapes are related? Draw or describe a way that works.

Paper Pinchers

Explorations with Sets of Folds

Measure and record the dimensions of the open square.
For each set of folds, bring the corners to the center.
Then measure and record the dimensions of the folded
square. Make three sets of folds and complete the
unshaded part of the table.

Fold	Length (cm)	Width (cm)	Area (cm²)
Open square			
1st			
2nd			
3rd			
4th			

Fold to find the center.   1st fold

Study the table. What patterns do you see?

Predict the dimensions and area of the fourth fold
without making a fold.

Paper Pinchers

Explorations with Origami

To make the base for each of the figures below, start with an open square. For each set of folds, bring the corners to the center. Then turn the square over and repeat the folds the number of times needed.

Servant

Make three sets of folds. Turn over. Open and flatten three of the small squares. Draw a face on the remaining square.

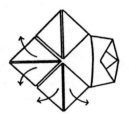 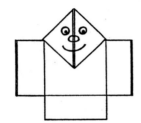

3-D star

Make two sets of folds. Turn over and fold each square back along the diagonal (A). Fold the whole figure along all lines of symmetry (B). Pinch the corner triangles into mountain folds (C).

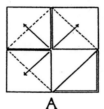 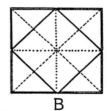 

A B C

---- *valley folds*
..... *mountain folds*

Fancy box

Make two sets of folds. Fold the triangles back (A) and make a mountain fold along the base of each triangle. Turn over and make the pleats (B). Pinch the triangle corners into mountain folds (C). Make a vertical fold from the center of the pleated border to the base (D) to form a box.

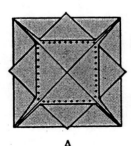 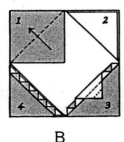 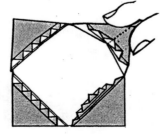 

A B C D

Challenge: Fold one of the figures using the smallest square possible.
What size was your paper? _____

Circle Sighs

Topic
Circles, radius and diameter

Key Question
What are the radius and diameter of each of your circles?

Focus
The students will use paper clips to draw circles, determining their radii and diameters.

Guiding Documents
Project 2061 Benchmarks
- *When people care about what is being counted or measured, it is important for them to say what the units are (three degrees Fahrenheit is different from three centimeters, three miles from three miles per hour).*
- *Tables and graphs can show how values of one quantity are related to values of another.*

NRC Standards
- *Employ simple equipment and tools to gather data and extend the senses.*
- *Use data to construct a reasonable explanation.*
- *Communicate investigations and explanations.*

NCTM Standards
- *Describe, model, draw, and classify shapes*
- *Relate geometric ideas to number and measurement ideas*
- *Develop the process of measuring and concepts related to units of measurement*

Math
Geometry
    circles
Measurement

Integrated Processes
Observing
Comparing and contrasting
Collecting and recording data
Interpreting data
Drawing conclusions

Materials
Part 1
    paper clips, jumbo and regular size
    large construction paper 12" x 18", 2 sheets per
        pair of students
    tape
    chart paper

Part 2
    paper clips, jumbo and regular size
    markers or colored tissue paper, white glue, and
        paint brushes (see *Management 1*)

Background Information
Before students begin to use compasses and protractors, they should be given time to explore and enjoy the drawing of circles. In this activity they will use paper clips to draw circles and paper clip chains to measure the diameter and radius of each circle. Through the collection of data, students should reach the conclusion that the diameter is twice the length of the radius.

Management
1. This activity is divided into two parts. In *Part 1* the students will learn how to use paper clips to draw circles. They will collect and record data to determine the radius and diameter of each circle. In *Part 2* students will use paper clips to draw circles in interesting designs. They can then color their work or cut circles from colored tissue paper and adhere them to their drawings by applying a wash of white glue and water with a paint brush (one part white glue to two parts water).
2. Students should work in pairs with both taking turns drawing the circles.
3. Each pair will need 20 paper clips. They will use 10 chained together to make a measuring device with paper clip units (pc). The other ten will be used for drawing circles. For making comparisons, have some students use jumbo-size clips while others use regular-size clips.

Procedure
1. Ask the students how they could use a paper clip to draw a circle. As they are describing their methods, try to follow their directions on the overhead projector. If students do not arrive at the solution that is illustrated (or a better one), demonstrate how to place a pencil in each loop of the paper clip and trace a circle as they spin one end around the stationary pencil in the other loop.

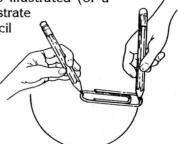

2. Inform them that they will be drawing circles on a piece of paper, along with measuring and recording the radii and diameters of the circles they have drawn. If appropriate, weave the story of the ranch hands riding from the rim of Circle Ranch to the resting place in the middle of the ranch for the radius measure and all the way across the circle, passing by the resting place, for the diameter measure.

3. Show the students a chain of paper clips. Inform them that they will be measuring their circles with a measuring device similar to this. Ask them what units they think they will record for their measures. [paper clip units, or pc]

4. Distribute a sheet of paper (scratch paper will do) to each pair of students. Allow them time to practice drawing the circles.

5. Distribute the large sheets of construction paper, two sheets per pair of students. Direct the students to tape one long edge of one sheet of paper to a long edge of the other sheet of paper.

6. Have the students devise a strategy for finding the center of the paper and draw a dot there. (They can measure; they can fold the paper in half horizontally and vertically and use the point of intersection; they can use a straight edge such as a meter stick to draw a line diagonally from one corner to the other and use this intersection.) Allow time for them to share their strategies and assist any who are having difficulties.

7. Distribute 20 paper clips to each pair of students. Have them chain 10 together as a measuring device and practice reading the length of items around their area. (For example, they can measure their pencil and report that it is three paper clip units long.)

8. After they have practiced measuring with their paper clip chain, direct them to use the center dot for drawing all their circles. Have them draw a circle using only one paper clip. Invite them to measure and record the distance from the center dot to the edge of the circle (the radius). Next, direct them to measure and record the distance from one edge of the circle to the other edge, making sure their measuring chain goes through the center of the circle (the diameter).

9. Continue this procedure of drawing, measuring, and recording through the use of two and three paper clips. Then ask the students to predict, without measuring, how many paper clips they will be able to use before the circle gets too big for their paper. Have them record their reasoning.

10. Allow time for the students to continue until they can no longer add paper clips for drawing circles and remain on the paper. (Those using the smaller paper clips will have more data to collect.)

11. When all circles are drawn, have the students compare their data, explaining why some groups drew more than others. Have them record any patterns in their data that they have observed. [The radius is always twice as long as the diameter.]

12. Challenge the students to determine the size of paper needed to draw a circle that has a radius of 15 jumbo paper clips or 20 regular clips. Once they have made this determination, invite them to use the appropriate amount of chart paper to actually draw the circle.

Part 2

1. Introduce some of the circle designs that are illustrated. Talk about the strategies for making them. Inform the students that the dots represent the middle of the circles they will draw. Allow students time to draw some.

2. Encourage the students to replicate a given design or create one of their own. Invite them to color their creations (or use the tissue paper/white glue wash).

3. Display their work.

Discussion

1. What is the radius of a circle? [It is a straight line from the center point of a circle to the circumference.]

2. What is the diameter of a circle? [It is a straight line that passes through the center point of a circle from one edge to the other edge.]

3. How are the radius and diameter of a circle related? [The diameter is twice the length of the radius.]

4. Will this pattern be different if you use the other loop on the paper clip? Explain. [No, the length between loops (the radius) is the same.]

5. How many circles were you able to draw on the construction paper? What does the difference in the numbers tell you about the paper clips? [We used two different sizes of paper clips.]

6. How are your circles alike? [They are all round. They share the same center—they're concentric.] How are they different? [The radius and diameter differ in each one.]

7. What patterns did you notice in your data?

8. What patterns do you get when circles of the same size are drawn so that their centers are placed on the circumference of another circle? What do you notice? What is the measure between centers? What about circles of different sizes?

9. What things did you discover when you were drawing your circle designs? Which designs do you want to explore further? Why?

Extensions

1. Have students symmetrically color their circle designs.

2. Have students research the five rings of the Olympic symbol and replicate them.

3. Investigate drawing circles using loops of string instead of paper clips.

Circle Sighs

For each circle, measure and record your data.

Circle	Number of Paper Clips for Drawing	Radius (pc)	Diameter (pc)
A			
B			
C			

Without measuring, predict how many paper clips you'll be able to use for drawing circles before you go off the paper.

How did you decide?

Finish collecting your data.

Circle	Number of Paper Clips for Drawing	Radius (pc)	Diameter (pc)
D	4		
E	5		
F	6		
G	7		
H	8		
I	9		
J	10		

What patterns do you notice in your data?

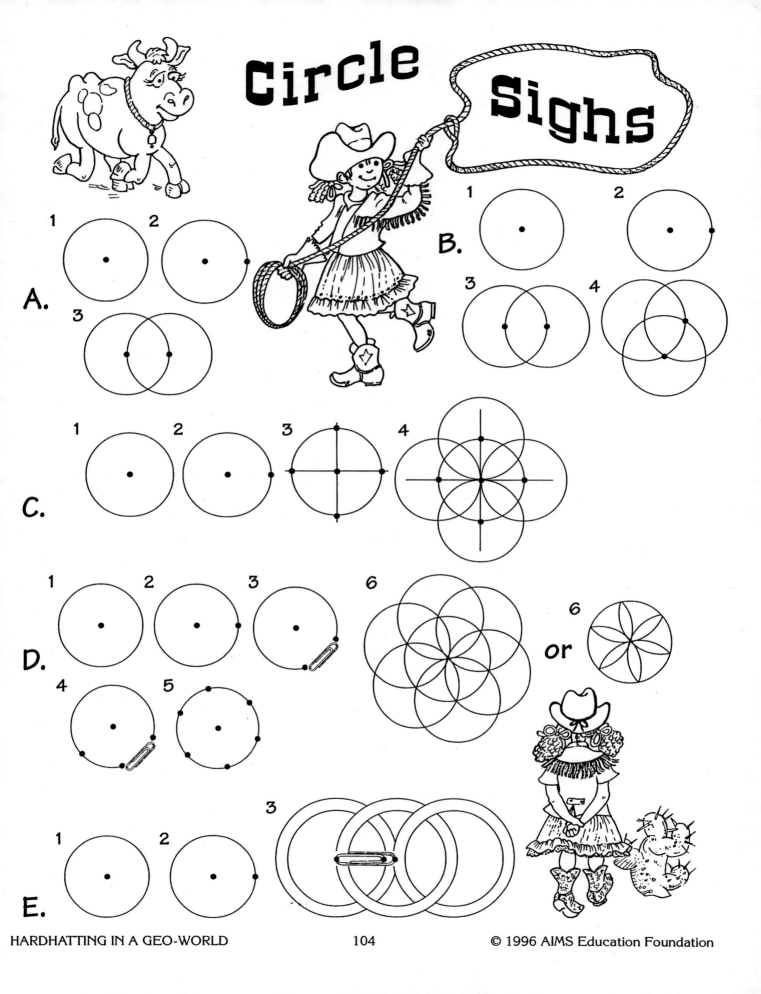

Circle Sighs

A.

B.

C.

D.

or

E.

Playground Geometry

Topic
Geometry/measurement

Key Question
Challenge: Find and measure squares, rectangles, and circles on your playground.

Focus
Students will expand their understanding of geometric shapes by finding and measuring parts of squares, rectangles, and circles on their playground.

Guiding Documents
Project 2061 Benchmarks
- *Shapes such as circles, squares, and triangles can be used to describe many things that can be seen.*
- *Measurements are always likely to give slightly different numbers, even if what is being measured stays the same.*

NRC Standard
- *Employ simple equipment and tools to gather data and extend the senses.*

NCTM Standards
- *Relate geometric ideas to number and measurement ideas*
- *Recognize and appreciate geometry in their world*
- *Make and use measurements in problems and everyday situations*

Math
Geometry and spatial sense
Measurement
    linear
Rounding
Whole number operations
    addition: perimeter
    multiplication: area

Integrated Processes
Observing
Grouping
Collecting and recording data
Comparing and contrasting

Materials
Meter sticks
Trundle wheels or meter tapes
Calculators

Background Information
We can come to appreciate the many geometric shapes in our environment by deliberately drawing our attention to them. And that is what students are asked to do in this activity as they focus on the school playground environment.

The tactile experiences involved in measuring length, width, diameter, etc. enrich students' concepts of these terms. It also allows them to look for relationships among the parts of shapes. For example, a radius is half the length of a diameter.

It is appropriate for students at this level to identify and measure circumference. Discussing the relationship of circumference to diameter or using circumference to find area should be deferred until they are older.

Management
1. Students should have previous experiences with length, width, perimeter, area, radius, diameter, and circumference before doing this activity. It could be used as a culmination or for assessment.
2. The whole activity can be done at one time or squares and rectangles can be done one day, circles on another.
3. You may wish to have each group record data on one activity sheet or for each individual in the group to keep a record of the data.
4. Choose whether you want everyone to measure the same objects or permit each small group to choose their own objects to measure.
5. If everyone is measuring the same objects, have each group start in a different place and rotate from object to object.
6. Finding the radius or diameter may not be easy unless it is marked or students know where the center of the circle is. If it is not marked and is on a flat surface, mark it for them with chalk. Otherwise they will need to approximate it.

Procedure

(The following is the suggested procedure to use if the whole class will be measuring the same objects. See *Management* for another option and modify accordingly.)

1. Challenge students to find and measure squares, rectangles, and circles on their playground. Take the class outside for some initial scouting. Encourage them to offer their suggestions, then agree on the objects to be used.

2. Distribute the activity sheet and measuring tools to each group. Have students record the objects to be measured. Draw out their understanding of terms. Example: "Describe a perimeter." [the distance around a closed shape; *peri* (around), *meter* (measure)]

3. Discuss the procedure for gathering data (rotation or every group on their own). Ask questions such as:
   - From where shall we start measuring thick lines—the outside edge, the inside edge, or the middle of the line?
   - How shall we round our measurements, to the nearest centimeter or the nearest meter? (Large areas like soccer fields should be rounded to the nearest meter, smaller areas to the nearest centimeter.)

4. Take the class outside. Have the groups measure and record their data.

5. Return to the room so students can do perimeter and area calculations.

6. For circles, have students create their own table or other way of recording data. One possibility is:

Object	Radius	Diameter	Circumference

7. Have groups go outside and obtain the circle data.

8. Hold a concluding discussion.

Discussion

1. What problems did you have while you were gathering data?

2. How do our measurements of _____ (name object) compare? Why might they be different? (Some students measured more precisely than others or from a different starting place on a thick line, etc.)

3. How is perimeter related to length and width? [length + width + length + width or 2 lengths + 2 widths]

4. What is another word for the free throw line? [diameter]

5. How does the radius compare to the diameter? Use data to support your answer. (The radius is half the diameter. For example,...)

6. How are perimeter and circumference alike? [*Peri* and *circum* both mean "around." They are both distances around a closed shape. Circumference is just a word chosen to represent a special kind of perimeter.] How are they different? [Perimeters have straight lines and circumferences are curved.]

7. While you were outside, what other geometric shapes did you notice?

Playground Geometry

Squares and Rectangles

Measure length and width. Calculate perimeter and area.

Object	Length	Width	Perimeter	Area

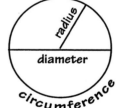

Circles

Measure and record the radius, diameter, and circumference of three circles.

Once Around the Track

Topic
Geometry: closed networks

Key Question
When can a network be traced without lifting your pencil?

Focus
Students will discover the two rules that determine whether a network can be drawn without lifting a pencil or retracing a line.

Guiding Documents
Project 2061 Benchmarks
- *Mathematics is the study of many kinds of patterns, including numbers and shapes and operations on them. Sometimes patterns are studied because they help to explain how the world works or how to solve practical problems, sometimes because they are interesting in themselves.*
- *Results of scientific investigations are seldom exactly the same, but if the differences are large, it is important to try to figure out why. One reason for following directions carefully and for keeping records of one's work is to provide information on what might have caused the differences.*
- *Offer reasons for their findings and consider reasons suggested by others.*

NRC Standards
- *Employ simple equipment and tools to gather data and extend the senses.*
- *Communicate investigations and explanations.*

NCTM Standards
- *Develop spatial sense*
- *Relate geometric ideas to number and measurement ideas*
- *Recognize and appreciate geometry in their world*

Math
Geometry and spatial sense
Patterns

Integrated Processes
Observing
Collecting and recording data
Comparing and contrasting
Generalizing

Materials
None

Background Information
A Swiss mathematician by the name of Leonhard Euler (1707-1783) was fascinated by networks and discovered rules that determine whether or not networks can be traveled. A network consists of a set of points or vertices connected by edges which may be straight or curved. A network can be traveled if it can be traced without lifting a pencil or retracing an edge.

Network	# of Even Vertices	# of Odd Vertices	Can it be traveled?
A	0	2	yes
B	5	0	yes
C	1	4	no
D	3	2	yes
E	0	4	no
F	4	2	yes
G	6	0	yes
H	0	6	no
I			

Euler's discoveries about closed networks relevant to this activity are:

1. *A network can be traveled if it has two or fewer odd vertices. An odd vertex has an odd number of edges or lines drawn from it. An even vertex has an even number of lines drawn from it.*

Odd Vertex   Even Vertex

2. The starting point sometimes matters. *To travel a network with two odd vertices, you must start at one of the odd vertices. You will end at the other odd vertex.* (Until students find this truth, there is likely to be a difference in some of their results. Encourage students to retest the networks where their results don't agree. It can give them a tremendous sense of accomplishment to find the key. This is also why it is important to mark the starting point.)

The number of even vertices has no effect on which networks can be traveled.

Management

Students should work individually but might discuss and compare in small groups.

Procedure

1. Distribute the first activity sheet and ask, "Which of these networks can be traced without lifting your pencil or retracing a line?"
2. Have students trace each network and write *yes* or *no* on the line by its identifying letter. They should draw and test a network of their own for letter *I*.
3. Give students the second activity sheet and ask the *Key Question*, "When can a network be traced without lifting your pencil?"
4. Explain that a vertex is a point where two or more lines meet. Review the definitions of *odd* and *even* vertices as illustrated on the sheet.
5. Have students complete the table, either individually or in small groups.
6. Guide the reporting of results (counts of vertices and networks which can be traveled) so students can make comparisons.
7. Students should retest networks where results differed. They should find that the starting point sometimes determines whether a network can be traveled or not (see *Background Information*). Their thinking should be recorded under the question, "Why might someone get different results?"
8. Have students study the odd vertices and write a general rule to answer the *Key Question*.

Discussion

1. What rule did you write? How did you test it to make sure the rule was a good one? (Students should try additional networks of their own to see if their rule holds true.)
2. What do you notice about the numbers in the odd vertices column? [They are all even numbers.] Will this always be true? [For closed networks, yes. (But challenge students to prove otherwise.)]
3. How many different networks that can be traveled can we find? (see *Extension*)

Extension

Start a bulletin board showing networks that can be traveled. Have students draw them on colored construction paper and glue yarn along the lines to add more color. As the display grows, challenge students to find new networks that can be traveled.

Once Around the Track

When can a network be traced without lifting your pencil?

Mark your starting point (vertex). Trace lines only one time.
Write **yes** if the network can be traveled, **no** if it cannot.

A

B _____

C _____

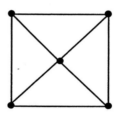

D _____

E _____

F _____

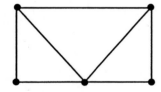

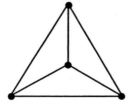

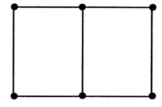

G _____

H _____

I _____

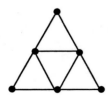

Draw
your
own.

110

Once Around the Track

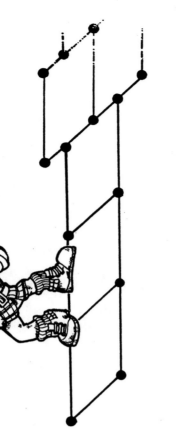

An **odd vertex** has an odd number of lines drawn from it.

An **even vertex** has an even number of lines drawn from it.

Network	# of Even Vertices	# of Odd Vertices	Can it be traveled?
A			
B			
C			
D			
E			
F			
G			
H			
I			

How do your results compare to others?

Why might someone get different results?

Look at the number of odd vertices in networks that can be traveled. Write a rule.

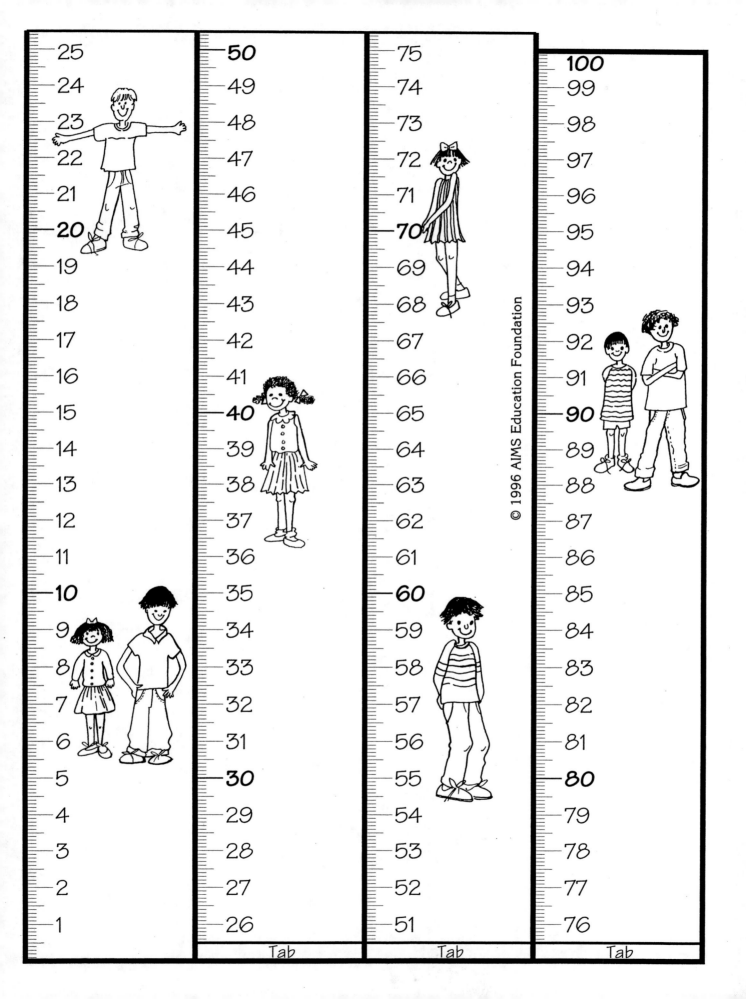

25
24
23
22
21
20
19
18
17
16
15
14
13
12
11
10
9
8
7
6
5
4
3
2
1

50
49
48
47
46
45
44
43
42
41
40
39
38
37
36
35
34
33
32
31
30
29
28
27
26

Tab

75
74
73
72
71
70
69
68
67
66
65
64
63
62
61
60
59
58
57
56
55
54
53
52
51

Tab

100
99
98
97
96
95
94
93
92
91
90
89
88
87
86
85
84
83
82
81
80
79
78
77
76

Tab

The AIMS Program

AIMS is the acronym for "Activities Integrating Mathematics and Science." Such integration enriches learning and makes it meaningful and holistic. AIMS began as a project of Fresno Pacific University to integrate the study of mathematics and science in grades K-9, but has since expanded to include language arts, social studies, and other disciplines.

AIMS is a continuing program of the non-profit AIMS Education Foundation. It had its inception in a National Science Foundation funded program whose purpose was to explore the effectiveness of integrating mathematics and science. The project directors in cooperation with 80 elementary classroom teachers devoted two years to a thorough field-testing of the results and implications of integration.

The approach met with such positive results that the decision was made to launch a program to create instructional materials incorporating this concept. Despite the fact that thoughtful educators have long recommended an integrative approach, very little appropriate material was available in 1981 when the project began. A series of writing projects have ensued and today the AIMS Education Foundation is committed to continue the creation of new integrated activities on a permanent basis.

The AIMS program is funded through the sale of this developing series of books and proceeds from the Foundation's endowment. All net income from program and products flows into a trust fund administered by the AIMS Education Foundation. Use of these funds is restricted to support of research, development, and publication of new materials. Writers donate all their rights to the Foundation to support its on-going program. No royalties are paid to the writers.

The rationale for integration lies in the fact that science, mathematics, language arts, social studies, etc., are integrally interwoven in the real world from which it follows that they should be similarly treated in the classroom where we are preparing students to live in that world. Teachers who use the AIMS program give enthusiastic endorsement to the effectiveness of this approach.

Science encompasses the art of questioning, investigating, hypothesizing, discovering, and communicating. Mathematics is the language that provides clarity, objectivity, and understanding. The language arts provide us powerful tools of communication. Many of the major contemporary societal issues stem from advancements in science and must be studied in the context of the social sciences. Therefore, it is timely that all of us take seriously a more holistic mode of educating our students. This goal motivates all who are associated with the AIMS Program. We invite you to join us in this effort.

Meaningful integration of knowledge is a major recommendation coming from the nation's professional science and mathematics associations. The American Association for the Advancement of Science in *Science for All Americans* strongly recommends the integration of mathematics, science, and technology. The National Council of Teachers of Mathematics places strong emphasis on applications of mathematics such as are found in science investigations. AIMS is fully aligned with these recommendations.

Extensive field testing of AIMS investigations confirms these beneficial results.

1. Mathematics becomes more meaningful, hence more useful, when it is applied to situations that interest students.
2. The extent to which science is studied and understood is increased, with a significant economy of time, when mathematics and science are integrated.
3. There is improved quality of learning and retention, supporting the thesis that learning which is meaningful and relevant is more effective.
4. Motivation and involvement are increased dramatically as students investigate real-world situations and participate actively in the process.

We invite you to become part of this classroom teacher movement by using an integrated approach to learning and sharing any suggestions you may have. The AIMS Program welcomes you!

AIMS Education Foundation Programs

A Day with AIMS

Intensive one-day workshops are offered to introduce educators to the philosophy and rationale of AIMS. Participants will discuss the methodology of AIMS and the strategies by which AIMS principles may be incorporated into curriculum. Each participant will take part in a variety of hands-on AIMS investigations to gain an understanding of such aspects as the scientific/mathematical content, classroom management, and connections with other curricular areas. *A Day with AIMS* workshops may be offered anywhere in the United States. Necessary supplies and take-home materials are usually included in the enrollment fee.

A Week with AIMS

Throughout the nation, AIMS offers many one-week workshops each year, usually in the summer. Each workshop lasts five days and includes at least 30 hours of AIMS hands-on instruction. Participants are grouped according to the grade level(s) in which they are interested. Instructors are members of the AIMS Instructional Leadership Network. Supplies for the activities and a generous supply of take-home materials are included in the enrollment fee. Sites are selected on the basis of applications submitted by educational organizations. If chosen to host a workshop, the host agency agrees to provide specified facilities and cooperate in the promotion of the workshop. The AIMS Education Foundation supplies workshop materials as well as the travel, housing, and meals for instructors.

AIMS One-Week Perspectives Workshops

Each summer, Fresno Pacific University offers AIMS one-week workshops on its campus in Fresno, California. AIMS Program Directors and highly qualified members of the AIMS National Leadership Network serve as instructors.

The Science Festival and the Festival of Mathematics

Each summer, Fresno Pacific University offers a Science Festival and a Festival of Mathematics. These festivals have gained national recognition as inspiring and challenging experiences, giving unique opportunities to experience hands-on mathematics and science in topical and grade-level groups. Guest faculty includes some of the nation's most highly regarded mathematics and science educators. Supplies and take-home materials are included in the enrollment fee.

The AIMS Instructional Leadership Program

This is an AIMS staff-development program seeking to prepare facilitators for leadership roles in science/math education in their home districts or regions. Upon successful completion of the program, trained facilitators become members of the AIMS Instructional Leadership Network, qualified to conduct AIMS workshops, teach AIMS in-service courses for college credit, and serve as AIMS consultants. Intensive training is provided in mathematics, science, process and thinking skills, workshop management, and other relevant topics.

College Credit and Grants

Those who participate in workshops may often qualify for college credit. If the workshop takes place on the campus of Fresno Pacific University, that institution may grant appropriate credit. If the workshop takes place off-campus, arrangements can sometimes be made for credit to be granted by another college or university. In addition, the applicant's home school district is often willing to grant in-service or professional development credit. Many educators who participate in AIMS workshops are recipients of various types of educational grants, either local or national. Nationally known foundations and funding agencies have long recognized the value of AIMS mathematics and science workshops to educators. The AIMS Education Foundation encourages educators interested in attending or hosting workshops to explore the possibilities suggested above. Although the Foundation strongly supports such interest, it reminds applicants that they have the primary responsibility for fulfilling *current* requirements.

For current information regarding the programs described above, please complete the following:

Information Request

Please send current information on the items checked:

___ *Basic Information Packet* on AIMS materials
___ *Festival of Mathematics*
___ *Science Festival*
___ *AIMS Instructional Leadership Program*

___ *AIMS One-Week Perspectives* workshops
___ *A Week with AIMS* workshops
___ Hosting information for *A Day with AIMS* workshops
___ Hosting information for *A Week with AIMS* workshops

Name _____ Phone _____

Address _____
       Street   City   State   Zip

AIMS Program Publications

GRADES K-4 SERIES

Bats Incredible!
Brinca de Alegría Hacia la Primavera con las Matemáticas y Ciencias
Cáete de Gusto Hacia el Otoño con la Matemática y Ciencias
Cycles of Knowing and Growing
Fall Into Math and Science
Field Detectives
Glide Into Winter With Math and Science
Hardhatting in a Geo-World (Revised Edition, 1996)
Jaw Breakers and Heart Thumpers (Revised Edition, 1995)
Los Cincos Sentidos
Overhead and Underfoot (Revised Edition, 1994)
Patine al Invierno con Matemáticas y Ciencias
Popping With Power (Revised Edition, 1996)
Primariamente Física (Revised Edition, 1994)
Primarily Earth
Primariamente Plantas
Primarily Physics (Revised Edition, 1994)
Primarily Plants
Sense-able Science
Spring Into Math and Science
Under Construction

GRADES K-6 SERIES

Budding Botanist
Critters
El Botanista Principiante
Exploring Environments
Mostly Magnets
Ositos Nada Más
Primarily Bears
Principalmente Imanes
Water Precious Water

GRADES 5-9 SERIES

Actions with Fractions
Brick Layers
Brick Layers II
Conexiones Eléctricas
Down to Earth
Electrical Connections
Finding Your Bearings (Revised Edition, 1996)
Floaters and Sinkers (Revised Edition, 1995)
From Head to Toe
Fun With Foods
Gravity Rules!
Historical Connections in Mathematics, Volume I
Historical Connections in Mathematics, Volume II
Historical Connections in Mathematics, Volume III
Just for the Fun of It!
Machine Shop
Magnificent Microworld Adventures
Math + Science, A Solution
Off the Wall Science: A Poster Series Revisited
Our Wonderful World
Out of This World (Revised Edition, 1994)
Pieces and Patterns, A Patchwork in Math and Science
Piezas y Diseños, un Mosaic de Matemáticas y Ciencias
Proportional Reasoning
Soap Films and Bubbles
Spatial Visualization
The Sky's the Limit (Revised Edition, 1994)
The Amazing Circle, Volume 1
Through the Eyes of the Explorers:
   Minds-on Math & Mapping
What's Next, Volume 1
What's Next, Volume 2
What's Next, Volume 3

For further information write to:

AIMS Education Foundation • P.O. Box 8120 • Fresno, California 93747-8120
www.AIMSedu.org/ • Fax 559•255•6396

We invite you to subscribe to AIMS!

Each issue of AIMS contains a variety of material useful to educators at all grade levels. Feature articles of lasting value deal with topics such as mathematical or science concepts, curriculum, assessment, the teaching of process skills, and historical background. Several of the latest AIMS math/science investigations are always included, along with their reproducible activity sheets. As needs direct and space allows, various issues contain news of current developments, such as workshop schedules, activities of the AIMS Instructional Leadership Network, and announcements of upcoming publications.

AIMS is published monthly, August through May. Subscriptions are on an annual basis only. A subscription entered at any time will begin with the next issue, but will also include the previous issues of that volume. Readers have preferred this arrangement because articles and activities within an annual volume are often interrelated.

Please note that an AIMS subscription automatically includes duplication rights for one school site for all issues included in the subscription. Many schools build cost-effective library resources with their subscriptions.

YES! I am interested in subscribing to AIMS.

Name _____   Home Phone _____

Address _____   City, State, Zip _____

Please send the following volumes (subject to availability):

_____	Volume V	(1990-91)	$30.00	_____ Volume X	(1995-96)	$30.00
_____	Volume VI	(1991-92)	$30.00	_____ Volume XI	(1996-97)	$30.00
_____	Volume VII	(1992-93)	$30.00	_____ Volume XII	(1997-98)	$30.00
_____	Volume VIII	(1993-94)	$30.00	_____ Volume XIII	(1998-99)	$30.00
_____	Volume IX	(1994-95)	$30.00	_____ Volume XIV	(1999-00)	$30.00

_____ **Limited offer: Volumes XIV & XV (1999-2001) $55.00**
(Note: Prices may change without notice)

Check your method of payment:

❏ Check enclosed in the amount of $ _____

❏ Purchase order attached (Please include the P.O.#, the authorizing signature, and position of the authorizing person.)

❏ Credit Card   ❏ Visa   ❏ MasterCard   Amount $ _____

Card # _____   Expiration Date _____

Signature _____   Today's Date _____

Make checks payable to **AIMS Education Foundation**.
Mail to AIMS Magazine, P.O. Box 8120, Fresno, CA 93747-8120.
Phone (559) 255-4094 or (888) 733-2467 FAX (559) 255-6396
AIMS Homepage: http://www.AIMSedu.org/

AIMS Duplication Rights Program

AIMS has received many requests from school districts for the purchase of unlimited duplication rights to AIMS materials. In response, the AIMS Education Foundation has formulated the program outlined below. There is a built-in flexibility which, we trust, will provide for those who use AIMS materials extensively to purchase such rights for either individual activities or entire books.

It is the goal of the AIMS Education Foundation to make its materials and programs available at reasonable cost. All income from the sale of publications and duplication rights is used to support AIMS programs; hence, strict adherence to regulations governing duplication is essential. Duplication of AIMS materials beyond limits set by copyright laws and those specified below is strictly forbidden.

Limited Duplication Rights

Any purchaser of an AIMS book may make up to *200 copies* of any activity in that book for use at *one school site*. Beyond that, rights must be purchased according to the appropriate category.

Unlimited Duplication Rights for Single Activities

An individual or school may purchase the right to make an unlimited number of copies of a single activity. The royalty is $5.00 per activity per school site.

Examples: 3 activities x 1 site x $5.00 = $15.00
9 activities x 3 sites x $5.00 = $135.00

Unlimited Duplication Rights for Entire Books

A school or district may purchase the right to make an unlimited number of copies of a single, *specified* book. The royalty is $20.00 per book per school site. This is in addition to the cost of the book.

Examples: 5 books x 1 site   x $20.00 = $100.00
12 books x 10 sites x $20.00 = $2400.00

Magazine/Newsletter Duplication Rights

Those who purchase *AIMS* (magazine)/*Newsletter* are hereby granted permission to make up to 200 copies of any portion of it, provided these copies will be used for educational purposes.

Workshop Instructors' Duplication Rights

Workshop instructors may distribute to registered workshop participants a maximum of 100 copies of any article and/or 100 copies of no more than eight activities, provided these six conditions are met:

1. Since all AIMS activities are based upon the *AIMS Model of Mathematics* and the *AIMS Model of Learning,* leaders must include in their presentations an explanation of these two models.
2. Workshop instructors must relate the AIMS activities presented to these basic explanations of the AIMS philosophy of education.
3. The copyright notice must appear on all materials distributed.
4. Instructors must provide information enabling participants to order books and magazines from the Foundation.
5. Instructors must inform participants of their limited duplication rights as outlined below.
6. Only student pages may be duplicated.

Written permission must be obtained for duplication beyond the limits listed above. Additional royalty payments may be required.

Workshop Participants' Rights

Those enrolled in workshops in which AIMS student activity sheets are distributed may duplicate a maximum of 35 copies or enough to use the lessons one time with one class, whichever is less. Beyond that, rights must be purchased according to the appropriate category.

Application for Duplication Rights

The purchasing agency or individual must clearly specify the following:
1. Name, address, and telephone number
2. Titles of the books for Unlimited Duplication Rights contracts
3. Titles of activities for Unlimited Duplication Rights contracts
4. Names and addresses of school sites for which duplication rights are being purchased.

NOTE: Books to be duplicated must be purchased separately and are not included in the contract for Unlimited Duplication Rights.

The requested duplication rights are automatically authorized when proper payment is received, although a *Certificate of Duplication Rights* will be issued when the application is processed.

Address all correspondence to: **Contract Division**
AIMS Education Foundation
P.O. Box 8120
Fresno, CA 93747-8120

www.AIMSedu.org/
Fax 559•255•6396